PICK YOUR BRAINS
about
ENGLAND

Leo Hollis

Illustrations by
Caspar Williams & Craig Dixon

CADOGAN

Acknowledgements

The author and publisher would like to thank
'guest editor' James C. White (aged 12).

Published by Cadogan Guides 2004
Reprinted 2004
Copyright © Leo Hollis 2004

Illustrations by Caspar Williams and Craig Dixon
Illustrations and map copyright © Cadogan Guides 2004
Map by (TW)

Cadogan Guides
Network House, 1 Ariel Way, London W12 7SL
info@cadoganguides.co.uk
www.cadoganguides.com

The Globe Pequot Press
246 Goose Lane, PO Box 480, Guilford,
Connecticut 06437–0480

Design and typesetting by Mathew Lyons
Printed in Italy by Legoprint

A catalogue record for this book is available
from the British Library
ISBN 1-86011-158-0

Contents

Not to scale!

Vital Facts
and Figures

Do you know where England is? Look at Europe and then look up and to the left a bit. There is a small collection of islands, the British Isles. All these islands, except the southern part of Ireland, are in the United Kingdom (UK). England is the largest country in the UK, which also includes Wales, Scotland and Northern Ireland.

☞ England is separated from the continent by the Straits of Dover and the English Channel.

☞ The UK is a collection of 6,100 islands, of which only 291 are inhabited.

☞ At its nearest point, France is only 33 km (21 miles) away across the English Channel.

☞ England and Wales, including their islands, have a coastline of 5,214 km (3,240 miles).

☞ The total area of England is 130,439 sq km (50,363 sq miles), which is 70 times smaller than the USA.

☞ The total population of England is 48 million (approx.).

☞ The average age is 38.4 years old.

☞ 18.3 per cent of the population are under 14 years old.

Identity Crisis

There are so many different names that 'England' can be a bit confusing. What exactly is 'the United Kingdom'? What is the

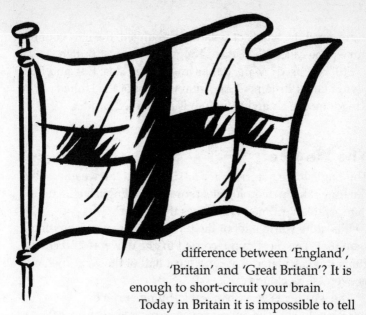

difference between 'England',
'Britain' and 'Great Britain'? It is
enough to short-circuit your brain.

Today in Britain it is impossible to tell
the difference between one nation's people
and another's. They have lived together for so long.

There are some clues in people's surnames: 'Owen',
'Jones' and 'Gwyn' are Welsh; almost everything with a
'Mac' or 'Mc' in it comes from Scotland or Ireland. But most
people have parents or grandparents who come from
different places within the UK.

Since 1801 the 'Union Jack ' has been the national flag that
symbolizes this combination of nations: the red cross of St
George; the diagonal red cross (or 'saltire') of St Patrick of
Ireland; and the white diagonal cross (or 'saltire') of
Scotland's patron saint St Andrew. Wales is not included
because at the time it was considered to be part of England.

'England' is a name that comes from the Anglo-Saxon
period, more than 1,000 years ago. The whole island,
including Wales and Scotland, is called Great Britain. Wales
was conquered by England in the 13th century. The name
'Great Britain' began to be used after 1707, when Scotland was
united with England. In 1801, when Great Britain and (in

those days) the whole of Ireland were united, the new country came to be called 'the United Kingdom' – or just Britain.

Still confused? Many adults are too. Try this: England is part of Great Britain; Great Britain is part of the United Kingdom; the United Kingdom is also called Britain.

The Weather

The English are notorious for talking about the weather all the time. The meteorologist's term for the English climate is 'temperate maritime'. What does that mean?

It is quite warm a lot of the time and wet even more times than that. The most rain recorded in one day was 27.9 cm, in 1955! It is calculated that for almost half of the year England is overcast by clouds.

The weather is very changeable. Summer can be refreshingly hot. The hottest day ever recorded was in 2003, when it reached 38.5 °C at Brogdale, near Faversham in Kent.

Because Great Britain is an island, nowhere is too far from the sea and this exerts a strong influence on the weather. Warm water, called the Gulf Stream, moves across the Atlantic from Mexico, which warms up the southwest coast. That's why you can find palm trees in Devon and Cornwall.

What is the Country Like?

Although it is a very small island, Great Britain is very varied. Whether you are looking for mountains, rivers, or even golden sandy beaches, they are all here.

There are many different types of landscape on the island. Much of England is cultivated farmland. This is 'the green and pleasant land' that the English poet William Blake wrote about. The farmland is mainly used for growing wheat and vegetables, and raising animal stock.

There are long coastal areas, such as the famous White

═ *The English Book of Records* ═

Did you know that some parts of the lowest area in the country, the Fens, are actually below sea level? Here are a few more of the most impressive things about England.

☞ **The highest peak:** Scafell Pike (Cumbria), 978 metres (3,210 feet) high

☞ **The longest river:** the River Severn (West Country), 354 km (220 miles) long

☞ **The biggest lake:** Windermere (Lake District), 14.7 sq km (5.7 sq miles)

☞ **The highest waterfall:** Cauldron Snout (Cumbria), 60 metres (200 feet) high

☞ **The tallest building:** 1 Canada Square, Canary Wharf (London), 235 metres (780 feet) high

☞ **The busiest airport:** London Heathrow, with 53.8 million passengers

Cliffs of Dover. Much of this is still untouched. Many people live near and make their career by the sea. Seaside holidays are some of the most popular in the country.

Most of the people live in the major cities and towns. London is by far the largest city and stretches over 1,600 sq km (625 sq miles), which makes it one of the biggest cities in the world. Other powerful cities, such as Newcastle, Birmingham, Leeds and Manchester, grew out of the Industrial Revolution in the 18th and 19th centuries, when factories attracted workers from the countryside.

The English Language

Did you know that 'bling' and 'phat' are accepted words in the English language? That is because they are in *The Oxford*

☞ Did you know that there are 470 airports in the UK? The main points of entry are Heathrow, Gatwick and Stansted, which are all near London. But there are also numerous flights to and from Bristol, Newcastle, Birmingham and Manchester.

☞ There are many ferries that cross the seas between England and Spain, Ireland, the Netherlands and France.

☞ The Channel Tunnel, which links Shakespeare Cliff in England with Calais in France, was completed in 1995. It goes 50 metres below the seabed. It is possible to leave London and arrive in Paris in less than three hours.

☞ The railway line through the Channel Tunnel was the only one to be built in (or near!) England in the 20th century, but the Victorians built 16,893 km (10,474 miles) of railway lines. Many have been closed down over the years, but most are still in use today.

☞ There are 371, 913 km (230, 586 miles) of roads in the UK. Around 75 per cent of families have at least one car.

☞ Concorde, the world's first supersonic plane, was designed by British and French engineers, and paid for by the British and French governments. It first flew in 1969. It could cruise at more than 2,160 km (1,350 miles) per hour, or twice the speed of sound! Since it stopped being used, in 2003, Concorde can now be seen only on the ground at Heathrow Airport, Bristol Airport and Manchester Airport.

English Dictionary (the *OED*).

The first English dictionary was compiled by Samuel Johnson in 1755. Today, the most famous dictionary, the *OED*, is so big that it covers more than 500,000 words in 20 volumes and runs to more than 21,000 pages. It weighs 61 kg. It is the last word on the English language.

When you travel around England you will find a number of very different dialects (local ways of speaking). In the north someone you have never met before might call you 'love', while in London you may be called 'china' for exactly the same reason (cockney rhyming slang: 'china plate' = 'mate')! In Newcastle they may just call you 'pet'. In the West Country they have a special name for visitors: 'grockles'.

There are also a few very funny phrases that the English use. Here's a selection:

☞ 'as cheap as chips' – not expensive

☞ 'a dog's dinner' – a mess

☞ 'hold your horses' – slow down

☞ 'in two shakes of a lamb's tail' – in a moment

☞ 'a sandwich short of a picnic' – mad (or stupid)

☞ 'that takes the biscuit' – That's extreme

☞ 'that's not my cup of tea' – I don't like it

What Makes the Nation Tick

England is one of the oldest democracies in the world. Although the monarch has always been the head of state, the real power lies in the Houses of Parliament, situated in Westminster in London. Both the House of Commons and the House of Lords have been running since the 13th century.

The House of Commons is attended by members of Parliament (MPs). At least once every five years there is a general election for the House of Commons. The Prime Minister is the leader of the party that gets the most MPs elected.

Most of the present Palace of Westminster was built in the 19th century, but there are parts of the building that are much older. On 5 November 1605 Guy Fawkes tried to blow up the building with King James I, the lords and all the MPs inside.

When the new palace was built, more than 150 years ago, it was not instantly a huge success. The bell in Big Ben broke, the hands on the clock were too heavy to move and there was no heating. It is difficult to run a country in these circumstances.

Today you can visit the House of Commons in action. It might look like a room of people shouting at each other, but that's democracy!

The Monarchy

On every stamp, coin and banknote you will see the crowned head of Elizabeth Windsor, one of the most famous women in the world. She is the latest in a long line of kings and queens that goes back

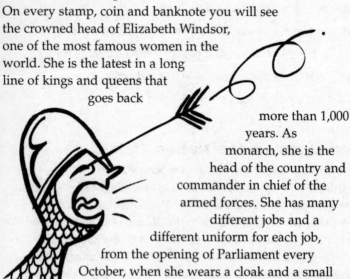

more than 1,000 years. As monarch, she is the head of the country and commander in chief of the armed forces. She has many different jobs and a different uniform for each job, from the opening of Parliament every October, when she wears a cloak and a small crown, to the Trooping the Colour, for which she wears a military uniform.

The history of the royal family has not always been one of brave generals and clever leaders, and some have even come to a sticky end. Poor old Harold II got an arrow in his eye at the Battle of Hastings in 1066. William II died after he had fallen off his horse. After Elizabeth I died, in 1603, they could not remove her white make-up even with hammers and chisels. Charles I was executed. George III, it was believed, went mad.

The Media

There are five major TV channels in the UK. Two of them are run by the BBC (British Broadcasting Corporation), which also runs five of the most popular radio stations. The BBC was started as a private company in 1922, but five years later it was taken over by the government. The BBC also runs the World Service and some satellite TV stations, which can be heard or seen all around the globe.

There are numerous local and national newspapers. *The*

January: New Year's Eve is celebrated everywhere, but what do the English do to see in the New Year? It is customary at midnight to join hands and sing the old Scots song 'Auld Lang Syne'. On New Year's Day there are  parades in many of the major cities. It is almost as colourful as Chinese New Year, later in the month, which is a wonderful noisy affair, with dragon dances, fire crackers and music.

February: One of the funniest events of the year is the clowns' service on the first Sunday in February. It is held at the Holy Trinity Church in Dalston, London, in memory of the famous 19th-century clown Joseph Grimaldi. The whole church is packed with clowns!

March: Crufts Dog Show is where you can see every type of hound, terrier and mutt competing for the prize of most pampered pet. St Patrick's Day, on 17 March, is as much about a pint of Guinness as it is parades in many of the major cities such as London, Liverpool and Manchester.

April: Many people put bets on the Grand National, the most popular horse race in England, which is held at Aintree in Liverpool. It is famous for the difficult fences that the horses have to jump – and for seeing who falls off. The boat race between the Oxford and Cambridge university rowing teams has been going on for more than 150 years. The teams compete over 16 miles up the River Thames. Thousands of runners compete in the London Marathon. The route takes in some of the most spectacular sights in London.

Did you know that the Queen has two birthdays? The Queen's real birthday is on 21 April, when there are gun salutes from Hyde Park. But later on 6 June, her official birthday, is marked by a military ceremony called Trooping the Colour. More than 1,000 soldiers march and parade for the Queen. The royal family end the day by standing on the balcony of Buckingham Palace for a celebratory wave to the crowds.

May: The football season ends with the FA Cup (see p.60).

The most long-established English sporting events occur between June and August. Together they are called 'the season'. They include the tennis tournament at Wimbledon; the cricket Test match at Lord's, where one game can go on for five days; the Royal Ascot races, where as much attention is paid to the hats that the ladies wear as to the horse races themselves; Henley Royal Regatta, which is a combination of rowing and drinking; and, finally, the sailing races during Cowes Week on the Isle of Wight.

August: Summer is also the time for parties and the most popular party in the country is the Notting Hill Carnival. The carnival was originally a celebration for the Afro-Caribbean community in London, but now that three million visitors come over the two days it is a national celebration of dancing, bright outlandish clothes and music.

October: The Queen opens Parliament after the MPs' very long summer holiday, while the Cockney Pearly Kings and Queens celebrate the Harvest Festival in London, where everyone dresses up in suits covered in buttons. You can guess which event is more fun!

In Nottingham you can find the ancient Goose Fair, which is almost 600 years old. It used to be an annual fair after the harvest, where everyone sold what they had farmed, including geese. Today, it is a fantastic fairground with all kinds of rides.

November: Bonfire Night, on the 5th, started long ago as a Celtic festival to mark the beginning of winter, but it is also called Guy Fawkes Night, because it was on 5 November that he tried to blow up Parliament. Huge fires are lit and fireworks are let off. There is also the traditional Lord Mayor's Procession in London, celebrating the arrival of a new mayor for the City of London. Remembrance Sunday is more sombre, as it honours the British and Commonwealth soldiers, sailors and airmen who fought during the two world wars and other conflicts in the 20th century.

December: In Trafalgar Square, London, there is a huge Christmas tree that is given to the people of Britain every year by the people of Norway, in memory of the help that the British gave them during the Second World War.

Times, the *Daily Telegraph*, the *Guardian*, the *Independent* and the *Financial Times* are more serious in content, and cover news from around the world. *The Times*, founded in 1785, is the oldest national daily paper. There are also the tabloid papers, such as the *Daily Mail*, the *Express*, the *Sun* and the *Mirror*. The *Sun* is the most popular paper in the country and sells approximately 3.4 million copies a day.

Although there is no Hollywood in England, they still make fantastic films, such as *Four Weddings and A Funeral*, *Notting Hill*, *Mister Bean* and *Bridget Jones's Diary*. Pinewood Studios, outside London, is where many of the biggest films, including the Bond movies, some of the *Star Wars* series and *Tomb Raider*, were filmed. Did you know that Inspector Clouseau in the *Pink Panther* movies may appear to be French but the actor who played him, Peter Sellers, was English?

English Humour

Who said that the English cannot laugh at themselves? They need a sense of humour for some of the things that they get up to! Most of them involve mud or creepy-crawlies. Here are some of the strangest things you can do in England.

Mudathon: a 200-yard race through mud that comes up to your waist, held in January at Maldon in Essex.

Cheese-rolling: a contest to roll a big cheese down a hill near Gloucester.

Lawnmower Grand Prix 12-hour Endurance Race: exactly as it sounds, but still very strange!

Pooh Sticks Contest: on the very bridge in Oxfordshire where Christopher Robin and Winnie the Pooh first played

Pooh Sticks in A.A. Milne's books, and as complicated as it looks (not very, then).

Biggest Liar in the World Contest: You need to be able to convince more people than just your teacher that you lost your homework at Holmrook in Cumbria.

Gurning contest: keeping up the old northern tradition of trying to pull the ugliest face, at different places throughout the summer.

English Place Names

From Bottom Flash to Middle Wallop to a village called Nasty: do people really live in places like these? The answer is yes!

Here are some of the stupidest place names in England.

- ☞ Hairy Side (Tyne and Wear)
- ☞ Pratt's Bottom (South London)
- ☞ Golden Balls (Oxfordshire)
- ☞ Hole in the Wall (Derbyshire)
- ☞ Willy Knot (Lake District)
- ☞ Dead Cow Point (Lundy Island)
- ☞ Foul End (Warwickshire)
- ☞ Loose Bottom (West Sussex)
- ☞ Buttock (Lancashire)
- ☞ Crapstone (Devon)
- ☞ Balls Cross (West Sussex)
- ☞ Dog Village (Devon)
- ☞ Great Snoring (Norfolk)
- ☞ Queen Camel (Somerset)

English History in a Nutshell

England is a pretty old country, so it is full of stories. Is it a 'sceptr'd Isle', as the playwright Shakespeare said? Will 'England, never, never...be slaves', as the patriotic song 'Rule Britannia' says? Is it just like the films, with people living in big houses? Or is it more like *Oliver Twist*?

George Orwell, one of the nation's greatest writers, believed that England resembled 'a family, a rather stuffy Victorian family, with not many black sheep, but with all its cupboards bursting with skeletons'. What can those skeletons be? What does the past tell us about this country?

Here are a few of the best stories about the nation's past that might, in a nutshell, help you to get to grips with England.

Prehistoric England

Did you know that Great Britain was not always an island? More than 50 million years ago it was attached to the mainland of Europe. Then it began to drift away into the

Atlantic Ocean. It is still moving today, but very slowly!

When they were building London the workmen kept on finding the bones of animals such as tigers and woolly mammoths, and even a rhinoceros! Where did these animals come from? When the English Channel froze over during what is called the Ice Age, many of the animals that one can now find only in Africa travelled to Britain. As the ice melted, about 9,500 years ago, the new inhabitants became stranded and made their homes on the new island. They are all now extinct.

Britain then became home to cavemen, who hunted animals in groups and lived in caves. Over the next 4,000 years they began creating local communities. About 5,000 years ago they started to build some of the ancient sites that we can still see today. The most famous is Stonehenge (see p.98).

Great Britain has always been a popular destination for visitors. For the next 2,000 years England was dominated by the Celts, who probably came from the areas that are now Germany and the Netherlands. The Celts learned how to use iron and build forts, and their tribes often fought each other.

The Romans are Coming!

The Romans tried to conquer the whole of the world that they knew about. Their empire stretched from Africa to Spain. But when they got to England they didn't find it easy to conquer. The famous Julius Caesar had a go and failed in 55 BC. Emperor Augustus postponed his attempt. Under another emperor, Claudius, the Roman generals first called off an invasion, but then succeeded in AD 43.

The Celtic peoples of England did not welcome their new visitors politely. The Roman historian Tacitus tells us that: 'They took no prisoners. They wasted no time in getting down to the bloody business of hanging, burning and crucifying.' Boudicca is one of the most famous of the English warriors who fought the Romans. She was Queen of the Iceni tribe, who lived in the Southeast of England. She supposedly rode a chariot that had knives on its wheels.

Yet the Romans quickly gained territory from Scotland to Cornwall. They stayed in England for about 400 years and laid the foundations for many of the major cities in England: Londinium (London), Verulamium (St Albans), Eboracum (York), Aquae Sulis (Bath) and Camulodunum (Colchester). They also made Latin, their own language, the official language of the country.

The Romans did lots of building while they were in England. They were famous for their very straight roads, long walls – in particular Hadrian's Wall (see p.125) – swimming baths and villas. Fishbourne Palace in West Sussex is one of the finest remaining examples of the Roman villa in England.

The Birth of England

The last Roman soldier packed his bags and left England in 409 AD and the English chieftains again began to squabble among themselves. As there was no longer anyone to defend the country, a number of European tribes began to cross the Channel. These tribes all had strange names, such as the Angles, the Saxons and the Jutes.

Their kings had even stranger names, such as Ethelred the Unready, Egbert and Athelstan. These kings set up seven kingdoms in England: Northumbria, Mercia, Wessex, Sussex, Kent, East Anglia and Essex. Alfred the Great was the first king to unite these kingdoms in defence of the whole of England in the ninth century.

When these kingdoms were not fighting each other, they were fighting the Vikings, who were not friendly at all. The Vikings included Danish forces, who conquered lands from Scotland to East Anglia and became kings of England in the 11th century. Cnut was the most famous Danish king. According to legend, he thought he was so powerful that he could command the sea. He placed his throne by the shore and ordered the tide to stop. Needless to say, he got very wet feet.

The Nasty Normans

For the Anglo-Saxons 1066 were a very bad year. They were conquered by a people called the Normans. Not a very frightening name, but at the Battle of Hastings they overcame King Harold II, who was unlucky enough to get an arrow in the eye and was then hacked into little pieces. As a result, William, Duke of Normandy, became William I, the Conqueror of England.

William I was very keen that the whole of England obeyed him. His army went around terrorizing the whole nation and he also ordered his officials to put together the Domesday Book, a report on almost every property in the land. This is an extraordinary record, including every child, ox, barn and field in the country. It can still be seen today at the Public Record Office in Kew, London.

The Norman kings lasted for nearly 100 years. They were succeeded by distant relatives from the Plantagenet family, which became the longest-serving royal family in England's history, spanning the years from 1154 to 1485. Most prominent among this family is Richard I, also known as the 'Lionheart' . He was a valiant warrior who spent most of his time on the Crusades, fighting to capture Jerusalem from the Muslim ruler Saladin.

Roses and Wives

The Tudors were by all accounts a funny family that ruled during a very important time in England's history. They won the nation in a civil war that has come to be known as the War of the Roses. This was not a contest about who had the best flowers, but a bitter 30-year struggle between two branches of the Plantagenet family, the House of Lancaster and the House of York, each represented by a rose: red for Lancaster, white for York.

In the end Henry Tudor of Lancaster won the crown at the Battle of Bosworth Field against Richard III. Legend says that not only did Richard poison the queen but he is also reputed to have imprisoned the two young princes, Edward and Richard, in the Tower of London. It was only 200 years later that they found the bodies of two young boys, buried beside the Tower in a box!

But that did not stop the Tudors being very nasty monarchs. Henry Tudor became Henry VII and his son was Henry VIII. He is famous for marrying six times! There is a rhyme that helps to remember what happened to his six wives:

Divorced, beheaded, died,
Divorced, beheaded, survived.

His second wife, Anne Boleyn, was said to have had 11 fingers. She was beheaded with a sword, which took three chops to finish off the job. She was the mother of Elizabeth I. Catherine Howard, his fifth wife, was executed after only two years of marriage. His last wife, Catherine Parr was the luckiest. By the end of his life Henry VIII was so fat that they had to use cranes to lift him in and out of the throne. He died in 1547. After he died, Catherine Parr married again.

Henry is also famous for changing England from a Catholic country to a centre of the Protestant faith. He did this for two reasons. He wanted to divorce his first wife, Catherine of Aragon, but divorce was forbidden by the Catholic Church, so he decided to start up his own church, the Church of England. He also wanted all the money from the English cathedrals and monasteries to fund his wars against France.

The Bloody Tudors

Henry VIII's three children ruled England one by one. Edward VI became King at the age of 9 and was always ill. He lived to the age of just 14. His sister Mary, who was a Catholic, was called 'Bloody Mary' because she ordered the burning alive of their leaders. Then

their younger sister, Elizabeth I, ordered the beheading of Mary, Queen of Scots, her own cousin! Elizabeth I is still one of the most celebrated of English monarchs. In her own time she was even given the nickname 'Gloriana'. Unlike her father she never married, so she was also called the 'Virgin Queen'.

The Elizabethan Age is sometimes called the Golden Age of England. It is the time of the plays of Shakespeare, the circumnavigation of the globe by Francis Drake, and the daring voyages of sailors such as Walter Raleigh. But not everything was as it seems. Drake and Raleigh were very adventurous seamen, but they were also pirates working for Elizabeth and attacking their enemies, the Spanish, who then ruled most of South America, and had lots of gold and silver.

The Revolting Stuarts

In 1603, the year of Elizabeth I's death, England and Scotland were united under the rule of James Stuart, the son of Mary, Queen of Scots. He was already James VI of Scotland. He now became James I of England.

It was to be nothing if not a bumpy ride for the Stuarts. Only two years after James came south to rule England, Guy Fawkes and other Catholics in the gunpowder plot of 1605 tried to blow his throne sky high. James's son Charles I was executed after the Civil War of 1642–49. James's grandson, Charles II, was only allowed to take the throne after years of exile in Europe, and then had to deal with the Plague as well as the Great Fire of London. Charles II's brother, James II, had to flee the country because he was so unpopular.

But it was an extraordinary century for the nation, in which Parliament slowly became the ruling power in the country. The English began to build up an empire as they travelled and traded abroad. This was also the era of the scientific revolution, in particular the age of Isaac Newton, perhaps the most famous English scientist.

You can't believe everything you see at the cinema! In 1608 a group of English sailors and merchants sailed from Devon and landed in North America. They soon encountered the native Indians. John Smith, the leader of the English settlers, was captured by the Indians, but was saved by the chieftain's daughter, Pocahontas, who persuaded her father not to kill Smith. She later married another Englishman, John Rolfe, and went with him to England, where she died at the age of 22. She is buried at Gravesend in Kent.

By George!

The first thing you would notice if you lived in the 18th century is that everyone who could afford to wore a wig, even the men. The hairpieces of the most respectable women could sometimes rise three feet above their eyebrows. You would also notice that these same women had very white skin. They hated sunshine and wore white make-up to show that they did not have to work outdoors. This was a great time to be a show-off!

The 18th century is also called the Georgian period. This is no surprise when you realize that all the kings from 1714 to 1830 were called George. There were four of them: George I, George II, George III and, yes, you guessed it, George IV.

This was also the age of exploration. Captain James Cook sailed around the world and discovered Australia. Unfortunately he came to a sticky end in Hawaii, where he was beaten to death on the beach by natives. Another great English seaman was Horatio Nelson. He was not a lucky sailor: he had one arm and one eye, and suffered from sea sickness. His famous last words were 'Kiss me, Hardy.' A statue of him stands on top of a column in the middle of Trafalgar Square in London, in honour of his victories.

All Work and No Play

It was also a terrible time to be at school. Being late for school or talking in class resulted in a beating with a strap. Even worse were boarding schools, where the children were sent away for months and could do nothing but learn lessons.

But that was better than working in a factory, where you could be fined for talking, arriving late or even whistling. If you were under 18 you might be expected to work for more than 10 hours a day. Young boys were also used to clean chimneys, unblock sewers and mend dangerous machinery.

During this period the United Kingdom became very rich by bringing produce from the many corners of the empire – cotton from India, gold from Africa, tea from China – to British factories, where they were made into things to buy. As a result the UK became the most powerful country in the world. But that does not mean that it was fun for everyone who lived there.

28

Have
you ever
heard of the Great Stink? By the 1850s almost half of the
nation's population lived in towns and it was impossible to
accommodate them all. Cities became desperately unhealthy,
particularly for the poor, and many dangerous diseases
killed thousands of people, because it was impossible to deal
with so much sewage. During 1858 the River Thames in
London became so smelly that people refused to open their
windows. Finally it was decided to do something about it;
proper sewers were built and clean water was provided.

The Empress

When Victoria was told as a child that she was to be queen
she said 'I will be good!' She reigned for 64 years. She was
not even five feet high (but was nearly five feet wide!), but
she had a terrible temper. She is famous for the phrase 'we
are not amused,' but the truth is that she never said it.
Perhaps it was just the way she looked.

Victoria was also called the Empress of India, although she never left Britain. She had an Indian servant called Abdul Kamir, who tried to teach her Hindi. She was not a very good pupil. Once, when her piano teacher told her to practise, she slammed the lid on his hands.

Victoria married her cousin, Albert, after she fell in love with him at first sight. But Albert died in 1861 and Victoria lived for 40 years in mourning. Many monuments were named after her husband, including the Albert Hall in London.

Victoria has been called the 'Grandmother of Europe' because many of her children married into the other royal and imperial families of Europe, including those of Russia, Germany, Austria and Greece. Even today many of the royal families are related in some way through Victoria.

The World at War

England ended the 19th century on top of the world. For the next 100 years the road was a bit bumpier.

The First World War did not take place in England, but it had a dramatic effect on the country. It was called the Great War. In August 1914 Britain declared war on the German Empire, which had invaded Belgium. Most of the British soldiers thought that they would be home before Christmas. They could not have been more wrong. The war dragged on for four years. In total 960,000 British soldiers were killed.

Once the war was over the world hoped that it had been the 'war to end all wars'. It was not. In 1939 Germany, now ruled by the Nazi dictator Adolf Hitler, invaded Britain's ally Poland, and Britain had to declare war. The Second World War was fought on many fronts and soldiers from throughout the British Empire fought in East Asia, Africa and Europe.

Hitler even tried to invade Britain. The Battle of Britain was a fight in the skies above Kent and Sussex. England was also extensively bombed. Huge areas of London and many other major cities were lost in the 'Blitz'. Nonetheless, under the leadership of Winston Churchill, who became Prime Minister in 1940, the British never lost their belief that they would win. On 6 June 1944 – D-Day – an attack on the beaches of Normandy was organized. Then the combined forces of the British, American and allied armies marched through France, Belgium and the Netherlands to Berlin, the capital of Germany, where they met their Russian allies and completed the defeat of Hitler's army.

The Nation that Swings (and Wobbles)

Six years of total war had done a lot for Britain, but left it an exhausted country that could not handle the vast responsibilities of empire. The British Empire became the Commonwealth as nation after nation gained independence.

The exhaustion soon turned into swing as the 1960s arrived and England become groovy. The Beatles and the Rolling Stones could be heard on every radio, and the 'baby boomers', the children who were born just after the war, brought a bit of colour back to the nation.

In the past 30 years Britain has increasingly become a European country, but it has always kept a special

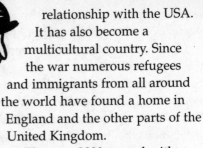

relationship with the USA. It has also become a multicultural country. Since the war numerous refugees and immigrants from all around the world have found a home in England and the other parts of the United Kingdom.

The year 2000 started with a bang around the world and England was no different, except it did not quite go to plan. Although there were many fantastic events to celebrate the millennium, such as the opening of the Eden Project in Cornwall and the building of the London Eye, two were not so successful. The Millennium Bridge, built across the Thames in London, soon got the nickname the 'wobbly bridge' because it began to bounce up and down, and had to be closed after just two weeks. (It is now safe to cross.) Also, the Dome in Greenwich was a massive disaster. It cost nearly £1 billion.

Mad Dogs
and
Englishmen

Here's a puzzle: What do Stan Laurel of Laurel and Hardy, Jerry Springer, Gillian Anderson from *The X-Files* and Charlie Chaplin have in common? They were all born or spent their childhood in England!

Who would you say is a typical Englishman? Is he a man with a bowler hat and an umbrella, sipping tea? Or a bold adventurer remaining calm under pressure? A groovy swinger, a talented footballer or a respected politician?

There are many sayings about the English: 'An Englishman's home is his castle'; 'Mad dogs and Englishmen go out in the midday sun'; 'The English are a nation of shopkeepers'; 'In Europe people have good food, in England they just have great table manners.' Which do you think is the most accurate?

The English have become famous in almost every area of endeavour, from wacky inventors to record-breaking sportsmen and women. Here are just a few of the most famous.

Great Britons

In 2002 the BBC decided to hold a competition to find the 100 Greatest Britons in history. Who was going to win? Would it be an inventor, a writer or a politician? English history is of full of heroes, and acts of bravery and daring: could it be someone who made an amazing discovery? In reverse order, here are the top 10.

10. Oliver Cromwell (1599–1658) did not have much of a sense of humour. He was one of the men who signed the death warrant of King Charles I. When Cromwell had his portrait painted, he told the artist to paint him 'warts and all'!

9. Horatio Nelson (1758–1805) was one of the greatest seamen to have been born in England. But did you know that he suffered from sea sickness?

8. Elizabeth I (1533–1603) is the only monarch to make the top 10 (see p.26).

7. John Lennon (1940–80) Born in Liverpool, he was a member of one of the most famous bands in history, the Beatles. Did you know that he and his wife, Yoko Ono, once decided, in a peace protest, not to get out of bed for a week?

6. Isaac Newton (1642–1727) is one of the most important scientists in history. The legend is that he discovered gravity when he saw an apple drop from a tree.

Sadly, it was a bit more complicated than that and involved a lot of maths.

5. William Shakespeare (1564–1616) wrote more than 37 plays. Most of them are still performed today and some have been made into films.

4. Charles Darwin (1809–82) spent more than 18 years studying barnacles! He is most famous for his theory of evolution, presented in his book *The Origin of Species*, which became known as 'the survival of the fittest'.

3. Diana, Princess of Wales, (1961–97) 'the People's Princess'.

2. Isambard Kingdom Brunel (1806–59) was an engineer. He designed the Clifton Suspension Bridge in Bristol, as well the largest steamship in the world, the *Great Western*.

1. The winner was **Winston Churchill** (1874–1965), the Prime Minister who led the country through the worst days of the Second World War. He is famous for his rousing speeches, which were powerful and, occasionally, very funny.

Brilliant Boffins and Bright Sparks

There were many English scientists who have changed the way we look at everything. There are also a number of extraordinary inventors. Inventions are sometimes created out of the strangest events.

John Harrison (1693–1776) invented a clock that told the right time. That may not sound like much, but it was the solution to the Longitude problem, which was crucial in shipping. Only by using an accurate clock can you calculate your position at sea and avoid shipwreck.

George Stephenson (1781–1848) was not the first man who made a steam engine travel along a track – that was **Richard Trevithick** (1771–1833), in about 1800. But it was Stephenson who started running regular passenger trains, pulled by engines that he designed himself. In 1830 his most famous engine, the 'Rocket', ran over and killed the Home Secretary, William Huskisson, although it was going at just 29 miles per hour.

Richard Owen (1804–92) may not have discovered the dinosaurs, but he did give them their name, which means 'terrible lizard'. He went on to found the Natural History Museum in London.

Humphry Davy (1778–1829) was a famous chemist who invented the safety lamp, which became vital in mining. It was the only way to light up the mines miles underground, where there was a great risk of explosions, and it helped to save thousands of lives.

You would not believe it by reading this inventor's name but **Thomas Crapper** (1838-1910) was actually a plumber who helped invent the flushing toilet!

The very first computer, the 'difference machine', was designed by **Charles Babbage** (1791–1871), but the engineers of his time found it too difficult to build. It was another English scientist, **Alan Turing** (1912–54), who developed the basic ideas behind all modern computers while he was cracking Nazi codes during the Second World War. The code-breaking that Turing and his colleagues did was kept secret until 1973, 28 years after the war ended.

Tim Berners-Lee (born in 1955) is the man who created the World Wide Web. Every time you see 'www.' on your browser it is worth thanking him. He gave the idea away for free, refusing to be paid for his invention.

Tall Tales and Scribblers

England has had a long history of famous writers and famous books. Here is a short history.

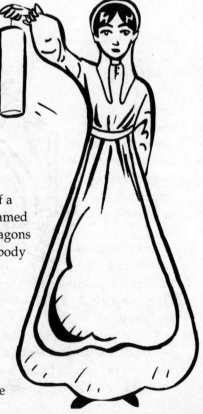

Beowulf, the earliest story written in English, was written more than 1,000 years ago. It is a long epic poem about a brave warrior who goes in pursuit of a murderous swamp monster named Grendel. It is a story full of dragons and blood-curdling feuds. Nobody knows who the author was.

The Canterbury Tales were written by **Geoffrey Chaucer** in the 14th century. A group of travellers who are going from London to Canterbury pass the time by telling each other stories. Some of them are serious and some of them are very rude!

There are a lot of famous playwrights, but none as famous as **William Shakespeare**. Almost every pupil will have to read some of his work at some point. But he can be a lot of fun. In particular, he invented some of the best insults in the world: 'Get thee away, base footballer' and 'Your brain is as dry as the remainder biscuit after a voyage'.

Robinson Crusoe was written by **Daniel Defoe** in 1719. It was based on the life of a real shipwreck victim, Alexander Selkirk.

Charles Dickens (1812–70) wrote many very long books, including *Great Expectations*, *Oliver Twist* and *A Tale of Two Cities*. One reason why these books are so long is that they were written in monthly instalments. The more Dickens wrote, the more he got paid!

The Hobbit also came from bedtime stories. **J.R.R. Tolkien** told his children stories based on things he had learned from medieval English legends. He made up some of the weirder stuff to frighten his children (but in a good way).

J.K. Rowling was born in England, but she now lives in Scotland. It is said that while she was writing the first Harry Potter book her flat was so cold that she had to write it in a café to keep warm. She is now the richest woman in Britain, even richer than the Queen.

Ladies First

Some of the best and longest-serving monarchs have been women: Victoria, Elizabeth I and Elizabeth II. It is no surprise that throughout history there have been some pretty amazing women who have made a difference.

Florence Nightingale (1820–1910) was known as the 'Lady with the Lamp'. She was a nurse during the Crimean War, when the British and the French went to war with

Russia. When she arrived at the soldiers' hospital she found no beds and no kitchen; rats ran everywhere and there was no ventilation. She brilliantly converted this death trap into a proper hospital.

'George Eliot' (1819–80) does not sound very much like a woman's name, but that is because her real name was **Mary Ann Evans**. She was one of the greatest novelists of the 19th century. She had to use a man's name for her novels because she lived with a man she was not married to, which caused a scandal in those days. Other famous women writers include **Mary Shelley**, who wrote *Frankenstein*, **Jane Austen**, who wrote *Pride and Prejudice*, and **Virginia Woolf**.

Emmeline Pankhurst (1858–1928) was the leader of the suffragette movement, which fought for the right of women to vote in elections. Many of the suffragettes including Emmeline even went to prison for their beliefs. Sadly, Pankhurst died just before she could see complete victory for her campaign when women were finally granted the vote in 1928.

Margaret Thatcher (born in 1925) was the first woman to become Prime Minister of the United Kingdom. She led the country from 1979 to 1990. She was born the daughter of a grocer. She was one of the most influential and controversial leaders of the time.

Up The Creek

The English have a habit of going to places where no one else would even think of going. This means that a lot of the nation's favourite heroes had very sticky ends.

Walter Raleigh (1552–1618) was an adventurer who was one of the first people to bring the potato and tobacco to Europe. Like coffee, tea and chocolate, they had never been seen in Europe before. Raleigh offered to go in search of the

mythical city of El Dorado, a
city made of gold, and
sailed up the Orinoco
River in South
America.
Unfortunately the
venture was a
disaster and he lost
everything,
including his son.
After he returned to
London he was executed for
being a pirate.

Captain Robert Scott ('Scott of the Antarctic')
(1868–1912) was the head of a team of explorers who tried to
reach the South Pole. When they arrived there they realized
that they had been beaten to the spot by the Norwegian
Roald Amundsen. The return journey was impossible
because the weather was so bad. The frozen bodies of Scott
and his team were discovered eight months later.

T.E. Lawrence ('Lawrence of Arabia') (1888–1935) was
working as an archaeologist at the beginning of the First
World War. He soon found himself working with the Arabs
in their war against the Turks, who ruled most of the Middle
East at that time. After the war Lawrence returned to
England and joined the RAF under an assumed name, but
he was never able to escape the past. He died in a tragic
motorcycle accident.

Baddies

Everyone loves a hero, but sometimes the baddies are just as
interesting!

Did you know that they never did find out who 'Jack the
Ripper' really was? As he brutally murdered his victims in

Victorian
East London,
the whole nation was gripped in fear. Some people think
that he was a mad doctor, others have even guessed that he
was the Duke of Clarence, the older son of Edward VII. We
will never know the whole truth.

There have been other baddies who have also gripped the
imagination. Robin Hood may have been an imaginary
character, but there were many like him who became national
heroes. There were highwaymen, such as **Dick Turpin**
(1705–39), who stopped coaches and robbed the rich.

The real stories behind these figures are slightly less
attractive. Dick Turpin was an Essex butcher who had bad
spots and even worse breath!

In the end, however, many of the worst villains were caught
by the police and their punishments could be grizzly. Every
attempt was made to make the death as painful as possible.
For the really nasty experience, it was even possible afterwards
to buy bits of the blood-soaked clothes of the victim.

After the criminal was killed the body was sometimes
hung up around the city on spikes as a warning. Later, the
body was taken away and sold to doctors, who could use the
body for experiments.

A Name to the Face

On every banknote there is a picture of the Queen. On the other side there is a portrait of a famous British person who has made an outstanding contribution. It is like carrying a bit of history in one's pocket.

On the five-pound note you can find **Elizabeth Fry** (1780–1845), who was a philanthropist and reformer. She was a famous campaigner for better conditions for the homeless and prisoners.

On the 10-pound note is the famous scientist **Charles Darwin**. When he published *The Origin of Species* in 1859, Darwin was ridiculed for saying that human beings evolved from apes, but he was right.

The purple twenty-pound note is slightly larger and features the English composer **Edward Elgar** (1857–1934). One of his first jobs was as conductor of an orchestra in a lunatic asylum! His most famous work, 'Land of Hope and Glory', was composed for King Edward VII's coronation, in 1902.

The fifty-pound note has a portrait of **Sir John Houblon**, the first Governor of the Bank of England. The bank itself can be found in London. It is sometimes called the 'Old Lady of Threadneedle Street'.

The Painted People of England

Nearly 2000 years ago, an Ancient English tribe called the Iceni used to paint patterns on themselves with blue dye.

Hey, my style's totally individual!

Trust me – next year everyone will be wearing this look!

Why did they do this? Maybe to scare their enemies, the Roman colonisers, who considered them savages.

Which was fair enough, really...

You want some?

Crikus!

London, 61AD

(Oh, that crazy woman's Boudicca, warrior-queen of the Iceni)

Over 400 years ago, Queen Elizabeth I used to whiten her face with lead-based make-up. She didn't know it was poisonous!

And in the 18th Century, posh women and men used loads of dodgy make-up to hide the disfiguring effects of rampant disease.

Greenwich Palace, London, 1588

It's a girl thing.

Darling, you look divine. But what's that horrible pong?

Carlton House, London, 1730

My nose is rotting. Is that a problem?

Of course, these days the English are so much more sophisticated...

Schmutter

TATTOO STUDIO

funky KIT

NEO retro

Camden Market, London, yesterday

tribe

...Right?

Local Customs: How the English Live

Time Off

According to a survey taken in 2000, the English spend at least half of each day eating, working, sleeping and watching television.

By far the most popular activity in England is watching television. More than 98 per cent of households have at least one set and each person is likely to watch, on average, for about 25 hours a week.

After a busy week at work, some English people like nothing more than a trip to the 'great outdoors' or to a visitor attraction. There are an estimated 6,400 attractions around the country and these can expect over 452 million visits a year. So it may be hard to choose where exactly to go. Here are the 10 most popular attractions in England.

1 Blackpool Pleasure Beach (Lancashire)

2 Tate Modern (London)

3 The British Museum (London)

4 The National Gallery (London)

5 The London Eye (London)

6 The Natural History Museum (London)

7 The Victoria and Albert Museum (London)

8 The Science Museum (London)

9 The Tower of London (London)

10 The Eden Project (Cornwall)

A Nation of Hobbyists

The English are passionate about their hobbies.

Some say that they love their pets more than their children. There are more than 14.5 million cats and dogs in the country, and their owners are willing to spend more than £3 billion on pet care every year!

There are a lot of very traditional hobbies and pastimes that you will not find anywhere else. Morris dancing is hundreds of years old. It can be seen in many towns and villages during the summer. Men dress up as horses, sometimes wear clogs, and dance with handkerchiefs and sticks. Other groups, such as the Sealed Knot, enjoy dressing up as soldiers and recreating old battle scenes.

Gardening has a long history on the island. For many people it is an obsession. All over the country it is possible to see stately homes with well-organized gardens. Some of these gardens also have mazes, which are almost impossible to work out. The most famous is at Hampton Court outside London, where the tall hedges make it impossible to see where you are going. But don't worry: at the end of the day a person always comes around to check that no one has been lost! (see p.82)

What are you saying?

So what is everyone talking about? Here is a quick dictionary to help you to understand what is going on. (*The Dictionary of Playground Slang* has more than 3,000 words and phrases in it.)

- ☞ **bad:** uncool; lame; pants
- ☞ **boy:** guy; lad; homeboy; fella
- ☞ **friend:** homechicken; mate; pal; brotha
- ☞ **girl:** chick; ladee; babe; bird
- ☞ **good:** wicked; nice; cool; safe; pukka; fab; phat; lush; brill; heavy; groovy; chilly wax
- ☞ **kissing:** tonsil hockey; sucking face
- ☞ **money:** kerching; bling; wad
- ☞ **toilet:** bog; lavatory; loo.

Text messaging is one of the most popular forms of communication. Here is a quick guide.

- ☞ **B4:** before
- ☞ **BTW:** by the way
- ☞ **CUL8R:** see you later
- ☞ **4EVRYRS:** forever yours
- ☞ **FYEO:** for your eyes only
- ☞ **GF:** girlfriend
- ☞ **HAND:** Have a nice day
- ☞ **sleb:** celebrity
- ☞ **Thx:** thanks
- ☞ **TXT:** text

Got to Have Faith

Did you know that in the 2001 census, 390,000 people claimed that they were Jedi?

Officially England is an Anglican nation and the Queen is the Head of the Church of England, but today it is a very diverse place. There are about 40 million people who claim to be Christians, including about nine million Catholics.

Places of worship can be found everywhere. There are now approximately 1.5 million Muslims in Britain, and mosques can be found in many of the major cities and towns throughout the country. There are about 350,000 Jews in Britain. The oldest synagogue, the Bevis Marks, built in 1701, can be found in the East End of London.

Just outside London one can find the first Hindu temple in Europe, the Sri Swaminarayan Mandir. Completed in 1995, it is the focus of worship for the 500,000 Hindus in the UK. It is built out of limestone and marble. All the stone was first shipped to India to be carved before the 26,000-piece jigsaw puzzle was put together on site.

Best Days of Your Life

☞ There are approximately 11.7 million children under the age of 16 in the UK. This is a greater number than the total population of many European countries, including, for instance, Sweden, Belgium, Greece and Portugal.

☞ There are 34,500 schools for 10 million pupils. About 92 per cent of pupils attend state schools. The rest go to private schools, which means that their parents have to pay for their education. English, mathematics and science are compulsory. Children are also encouraged to learn a foreign language.

☞ Many teenagers have some kind of part-time job. Fewer than half of the young population leave school at 16 to go to work straight away. It is against the law to have a full-time job if you are under 16 years old.

☞ Almost two thirds of children under 16 have TVs in their own bedrooms.

☞ Twenty-one per cent of children between seven and 10 years old drink at least 10 cans of fizzy drinks every week.

☞ People in England eat more sweets than in any other country in Europe. More than half of English children's pocket money is spent on confectionery.

☞ There are more than five million Sony Playstation™ 2s in the UK.

☞ Most families go on holiday together. More and more families are spending their holidays in the UK. More than a quarter of these are by the seaside.

☞ In a survey asking children where the most popular place to be is, 51 per cent said at a friend's house, 38 per cent said playing on the street and only 10 per cent said in a youth club.

☞ By the age of 13 more than half of all children have a mobile phone.

Planet Pop

The History Lesson

Who hasn't heard of the Beatles or the Rolling Stones? Forty years ago the charts around the world were filled with songs by English bands. But there is more to English music. Here is a whistle-stop tour through some of the most popular and bizarre styles.

Teddy Boys were the first rock-and-roll fans. They dressed very smartly in tailored suits. 'Teddy' refers to King Edward VII, who was renowned as a snappy dresser. The Teddy Boys were known for their drain-pipe trousers, brothel-creeper shoes and massive sideburns.

Mods were also fans of American music, but they made their style completely English. Their music was jazz. In the 1960s Carnaby Street in London was where they bought their smart suits, which were influenced by European tailoring. Their motto was 'clean living under difficult circumstances'.

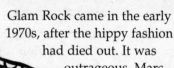

Glam Rock came in the early 1970s, after the hippy fashion had died out. It was outrageous. Marc Bolan, the singer of T Rex, wore make-up, glitter and platform shoes to shock the older generation. David Bowie was also famous for wearing a dress and pretending that he was an alien.

Punk was a reaction to everything that went before it. The energy of the movement can still be felt today in music by bands such as Slipknot, Nirvana and Marilyn Manson. The anger and the need to shock included wearing ripped clothes and using safety pins as ear-rings.

Pop Trivia

The artist who has had the most no. 1s in Britain is Elvis Presley. They include his 18th no. 1, 'A Little Less Conversation', which was a success years after he died, remixed by DJ JXL.

Pete Townsend, the guitar player for The Who, played so loud he went deaf.

The best-selling single ever is Elton John's song in memory of Princess Diana, 'A Candle in the Wind', which was originally a song about Marilyn Monroe.

The Sex Pistols' most famous song, 'Anarchy in the UK', was banned because it was rude about the

Queen. Yet it still went to number 1 in the charts!

The biggest concert ever held in England was Robbie Williams's gig at Knebworth in 2003. There were more than 400,000 people in the audience. Getting out of the car park at the end was a nightmare!

Festivals

Live music is hugely popular in England and there are venues in almost every town. But in the summer there are a number of huge festivals that can go on for days. Many of the world's most famous bands play at them.

The Isle of Wight Festival lasted for only three years (1969–71), but it was considered England's Woodstock. It was at this festival in 1970 that Jimi Hendrix played his last gig, before dying three weeks later. The same night Roger Daltrey, the lead singer of the Who, had a whisky-drinking contest with the legendary Jim Morrison of the Doors. Daltrey won!

Glastonbury is the most famous summer festival in the world. It was started by a farmer, Michael Eavis, on his own land. It is so popular that the thousands of tickets sell out in 24 hours. Usually held on the last weekend of June, it has bands playing every type of music, as well as films and every type of hippy therapy going.

Reading Festival takes place during the Bank Holiday weekend in August. It is famous for its rock music. It is said that the first time it was held, in 1971, there were more policemen in the audience than music lovers. Today it hosts many of the biggest names in rock, from Slipknot to Marilyn Manson and Beck. The same bands usually also play at the Leeds Festival on the same weekend.

A Little Bit of Sport

Footie I

Bill Shankly, the legendary manager of Liverpool, once said: 'Football is not a matter of life and death... it is more important than that!'

A long time ago football was played only on special holidays. All the men of the village would fight and scrum to get the ball from one end of the village to another. Sometimes the games were very violent and could go on for hours. Thankfully, it is a bit more civilized today!

Football as we now know it, with a pitch and goal posts, was first played in the 19th century. It began as an amateur team game. It was only in the 20th century that the sport became fully professional and all players were paid to play.

The FA Cup Final is the summit of the football year and comes near the end of the season in May. It is a competition that is open to any team that wants to enter. Started in 1872, it was the first football competition in the world.

Footie II

The most famous clubs in the country are Arsenal, Manchester United and Liverpool. Here is a quick history of the clubs.

Arsenal was founded in 1886, when a group of workers from the Woolwich Arsenal, an armaments factory, decided to form a team. They were originally called the Dial Square. They are nicknamed the 'Gunners' because of the military connection. They won their first match 6–0! It was only in 1913 that the team moved to Highbury, its present home, in North London. The team has been in the top division since it was invented.

Newton Heath LYR began playing in 1878. The players were all workers on the Lancashire and Yorkshire Railway. The club was always very poor until, by chance, a brewery owner, John Henry Davies, found the dog belonging to the team captain, Harry Stafford. Having heard the club's story, Davies decided to invest in the team if it agreed to change its name to Manchester United.

Liverpool was a professional club from the start. The very first team were actually all players from Scotland, so it was known as the 'team of all the Macs'. Liverpool fans are famous for adopting the song 'You'll Never Walk Alone', from the musical *Carousel*, as their main chant.

Messing About in the Sun

Does anyone understand the rules of cricket?

There are two teams of 11 people. While one team fields, the other bats. The fielding team has 11 players on the pitch and there are only two batsmen at any time. The bowler hurls the ball from one end of the wicket towards the batsman. The aim of the batsman is to try and get some runs. Confused? You should be!

Where can you find a square leg, a silly mid-on, a deep third man? These are all fielding positions in cricket.

Do you know how get a batsman out? He can be bowled, caught, leg before wicket or run out.

Croquet looks like a very relaxed game, but it can be very vicious. You have to hit a ball through six hoops. It sounds easy, but there is much more to it than meets the eye.

Newquay in Cornwall is the surfing centre of England. Surfing is a new sport for England compared to some of the more

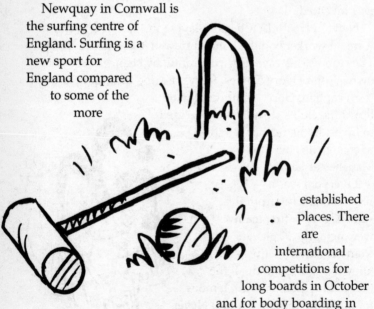

established places. There are international competitions for long boards in October and for body boarding in August. There are also great surfing beaches in North Devon, South Wales and even Northumberland.

Getting Stuck in the Mud

In 2003 England won the World Cup in rugby union. It was the first time that an English team had won such a prize in any sport since 1966, when England won the Football World Cup.

It is said that rugby was invented when a schoolboy, William Webb Ellis, got bored while playing football. He decided to pick up the ball and run to the goal. The school he was at was called Rugby!

There are two types of rugby in England. Rugby union teams have 15 players, but rugby league, which is played mainly in the north of England, has only 13 players in each team.

Hockey is a popular alternative to football in the winter. It was invented in England in the 19th century and can be played by men and women. There are more than 1,500 hockey clubs in England.

Because there is not much snow in England and few mountains, there is very little skiing. Most people go to France, Austria and Switzerland. It is even possible to get a train from London that leaves at night, so that in the morning you arrive among the Alps!

Food, Glorious Food

Not for the Fainthearted

If you happen to be a vegetarian, you will be lucky to avoid all this stuff but, believe it or not, the English would pretty much eat every part of an animal they could, including offal (the innards and guts of animals), roast bone marrow and pigs' tails. You name it and you can find it on an English menu!

Have you ever tried brains and bacon? What about braised oxtail? Jellied eel, anyone? How about the cooked tongue of a calf, sliced and put inside a sandwich? Is there nothing more appetizing than prising out a winkle from its shell with a toothpick and chomping down on something that looks like grainy snot? Do you know what Mulligatawny is? How do you make Brown Windsor Soup?

Course by Course

On most mornings busy workers don't have time for anything but toast, cereal and perhaps some fruit juice, but there is nothing like a full English breakfast to give you a boost for the day, or perhaps just stomach ache. But that is not all.

There could also be black pudding, fried kidneys, kedgeree or even kippers. Black pudding, which originally came from the north, is a sausage made up of pig's blood and spices that is then fried. But the fishiest of the lot is kippers: smoked herring from the North Sea. The fish arrives, blackened, at the table with its head still on. It has been steamed and you eat it with a knob of butter. But be careful, the flavour might remain in your mouth for the rest of the day!

Did you know that the sandwich was invented one night in 1762? The Earl of Sandwich was playing cards with some friends and did not want to leave the gambling table. He ordered his servant to bring him some beef but to put it between slices of bread, so that he wouldn't get his hands dirty!

Did you know that the nation's most popular fast food is not burgers but fish and chips?

Throughout the north of England there is no better meal in the week than Sunday lunch, and in particular roast beef with Yorkshire pudding, potatoes and horseradish sauce. The Yorkshire pudding is like a pancake that rises in the pan and is perfect with gravy and the sharp, bitter relish of horseradish.

The English love to add sauces or preserves to their meat. With pork they eat apple sauce. With ham they have English mustard, which can sometimes blow the top of your head off if you eat too much. Mint sauce goes with roast lamb, Cumberland sauce with game and cranberry sauce with turkey. All these meats can also be eaten cold, accompanied with chutney.

Kent, in the southeast, is regularly called the 'Garden of England', because so  many types of fruit are grown there. But did you know that the nation's favourite fruit is in fact the banana?

Throughout the summer you can find numerous very fresh fruit. Did you know that at Wimbledon tennis tournament in June/July, more than 270,000 tons of strawberries and cream are eaten in just two weeks?

Chocolate, the favourite type of confectionery, was first introduced in the 17th century as a medicine. It was sold in chemists' shops. Today it is estimated that the English eat half a million tonnes of chocolate every year!

The Cuppa

In times of trauma and anxiety most English people reach for the kettle and the teapot. Tea is the petrol that makes England run, but this was not always true.

The history of tea-drinking began in China about 1,300 years ago. But it was only in the 16th century, when Elizabeth I was on the throne in England, that tea arrived in Europe. It arrived in England about 100 years later. Tea mania swept across the country. At first tea was so expensive that people kept it locked up in boxes called tea caddies, but as more ships arrived back from the East tea became a national institution.

In any well-stocked grocery store you can see a huge variety of tea. Perhaps the most famous is Earl Grey, named after Charles Grey, the 2nd Earl Grey, who was Prime

Minister between 1830 and 1834. It is said that he was given the secret of the brew by a friendly Chinese mandarin whose life he had helped to save.

England's Favourite Food

In 2002, 430 million restaurant meals were served in Britain. Many of these offered more than just traditional English food. In fact, going out to eat can give you a chance to sample every type of food from all over the world. In London restaurants offer 170 different types of cooking.

Today the most popular dish is a mild chicken curry. The curry is an English invention inspired by Indian food. It derives from the word *kari*, which means sauce. Curry houses can be found in all the major cities and are particularly good in the areas where Indians, Pakistanis and Bangladeshis have made their homes, such as the East End of London, Leicester, Bradford and Birmingham. The balti is especially English. It was invented in  Birmingham. The Balti refers to the curved metal bowl that the meat is cooked in.

Chinese people have been visiting England since the 17th century. Many traders settled here in the 19th century. China offered more than just tea. Small Chinese communities sprang up over the years near the ports, bringing their own flavours to the multicultural mixture. Soon each major city had its own Chinatown. In London, Newburgh Street is ablaze with colour at the Chinese New Year in late January.

Many Italians moved to England after the Second World War, looking for work, and many of them settled here. They brought with them all the best of Italian food. Before they came you could buy olive oil at chemists' shops, not to use in cooking but to try to cure constipation!

London
Calling

The Name Game

Many of London's place names are very old and some started even before the Romans. London comes either from 'Londino's Place', after a Celtic king, or from old words for 'boat' and 'river', indicating that the city began as a place to cross the River Thames.

Here are a few of the most famous places in London. Can you guess where the names comes from?

A Piccadilly

B Oxford Street

C Trafalgar Square

D Knightsbridge

A: Piccadilly comes from 'Picadils', which were stiff collars that fashionable men used to wear in the 17th century. They were made by a tailor named Robert Baker, who had a shop in what is now Piccadilly.

B: This used to be called Tyburn Road, because it was the route that criminals would take towards the Tyburn tree at Marble Arch, where they were hanged. In the 19th century they decided to change the name to make it more attractive for shoppers!

C: Trafalgar Square was built in celebration of the Battle of Trafalgar (1805). Trafalgar is in fact in Spain.

D: There used to be a bridge here over the River Westbourne and it is said that a knight had a fight here.

'He who is tired of London is tired of life,' said the writer Samuel Johnson. It can take more than a lifetime to really get to know London. Today it is a 24-hour city, with a population of more than seven million people.

☞ One in every eight British citizens lives in London.

☞ Approximately 300 different languages are spoken in the city.

☞ One in four Londoners is a member of an ethnic minority.

☞ The whole city covers 1,600 sq km (625 sq miles).

☞ One in every five workers in London works in a bank or in other financial services, making London one of the financial centres of the world.

Building the City

London has been the home and work place of millions of people for more than 2,000 years. Each generation has left its mark on the city. Today there are 18,000 listed buildings, and 151 historic buildings and ancient monuments, meaning that they have been preserved especially for their historic interest.

The Roman remains in London include part of the original Roman Wall, in the Barbican, and the **Temple of Mithras** on Queen Victoria Street.

The Tower of London was started by William the Conqueror. It has been a palace, a fortress and a jail. It was in the Tower that many people were tortured and executed,

and then their heads were put on spikes to warn others! This is perhaps why one of the towers, built in the 15th century, is called The Bloody Tower.

Westminster Abbey was started in the 13th century, on top of the remains of an older abbey, but the building was not completed until 500 years later. At 31 metres (102 feet), its nave is the tallest in England. Every coronation since 1066 has taken place in Westminster Abbey.

St Paul's Cathedral rose out of the ashes of the Great Fire of London in 1666, when almost all of the city was burnt down. It took Christopher Wren until 1708 to complete the building. It was the first domed cathedral in England. Wren also rebuilt many of the city churches, and parts of the royal palaces at Hampton Court and Greenwich. He is considered the genius who rebuilt London as we see it today.

Buckingham Palace, built by John Nash, has not always been the home of the royal family. It was bought by George III for his son, but it was not used as the official home of the monarch until Queen Victoria moved in, in 1837. Nash also designed **Regent Street** and Regent's Park.

The Victorian age was the era of the railways. They built their stations to look like palaces, in honour of the power of steam. **St Pancras** is a perfect example of this fairy-tale design, which is called Gothic. This revived the old Gothic style of the Middle Ages. Also see the **Houses of Parliament**, **Victoria and Albert Museum** and the **Natural History Museum**.

After the Blitz, when the Nazi air raids devastated much of the city, there were huge spaces left open for new buildings. This was the age of the concrete block. There is nowhere more 'blocky' than the **South Bank Centre**, started in 1951 for the Festival of Britain that year by Denys Lasdun.

Today, English architects are some of the most exciting in the world. Much of their work can be found in the financial district of the City of London. In particular, Norman Foster designed the **Gherkin** (as it has now been nicknamed) at 30 St Mary Axe and the new **London Assembly** headquarters by Tower Bridge.

Going Underground

London is a huge city, but it is very easy to navigate if you know how. There are 329 km (204 miles) of underground track, with 292 stations; 18,300 licensed taxis; and 649 bus routes.

The London Underground is better known as the 'Tube'. It is an amazing network of lines that cross London in every direction. The Central Line is the longest line and reaches 54 km (34 miles). When the Northern Line goes underneath the Thames at Waterloo it is 67 metres (220 feet)

underground. The District Line carries more than 180 million people a year!

Every taxi driver in a black cab needs to have learned the 'knowledge'. This can take a few years. Before they are allowed to get a licence all drivers must be tested to make sure that they know every street in London!

The M25 is the motorway that rings the whole of London. It is used by 170,000 cars a day and is known as one of the longest traffic jams in the country!

The Lungs of the City

Nearly 40 per cent of London is made up of parks and green spaces.

A walk around Hyde Park and Kensington Gardens:

☞ **The Serpentine** is a lake at the centre of Hyde Park. Every Christmas morning the Serpentine Swimming Club have a race along the lake. There is a statue of Peter Pan by the Long Water.

☞ In 1851 people came from all over the world to see the Great Exhibition in Hyde Park. Organized by Queen Victoria's husband, Prince Albert, the whole exhibition was shown inside the **Crystal Palace**, built by Joseph Paxton. The palace was made completely from cast iron and glass, and was 1,851 feet long and 450 feet wide. Unfortunately, after it was moved piece by piece to Sydenham in South London, it was burned down in 1936.

☞ Every Sunday people go to make speeches at **Speaker's Corner**, near Marble Arch. This is an ancient tradition, as it was one of the few places one could speak freely without worry from the police. Even today speakers from every religion and persuasion try and shout above the noise.

☞ **Kensington Palace**, as seen today, was designed by Christopher Wren. It used to be the home of Princess Diana.

☞ **The Albert Memorial** is a glittering gold spire that Queen Victoria built in honour of her husband after his death. It stands opposite the Albert Hall, which was built at the same time.

Squares, Circuses and Cemeteries

Many of the buildings in London are built around squares or circles. It is not hard to see why they are called squares (which usually also have small gardens in the middle) and circuses (which don't).

Trafalgar Square is a ceremonial centre that was created to hold Nelson's Column, in memory of the great Admiral. In the northwest corner, in front of the National Gallery, there is a statue missing. They are trying to decide what to put there. What do you think would be appropriate?

Piccadilly Circus is famous for the Eros statue, which was put there in memory of Lord Shaftesbury. The only problem is that it is facing in the wrong direction. It was originally supposed to point up Shaftesbury Avenue. Instead it shows the street its bottom!

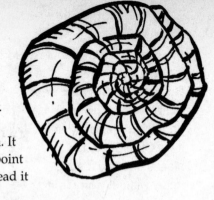

For the ghoulishly minded there are lots of fabulous cemeteries, such as at Highgate in the north and Kensal Green in the west of the city. Many famous people have been buried in them. But the scariest burial grounds are in fact unmarked! During the Great Plague of 1665, which killed thousands of Londoners, the dead were thrown into pits. These now lie under the ground opposite the Victoria and Albert Museum, near Carnaby Street in Soho and near Harrod's in Knightsbridge.

Museums

There are more than 200 museums in London. They include the Old Operating Theatre, Borough, where they used to cut people open; the Hunter Collection in Lincoln's Inn Fields, which has the skeleton of a giant; and the underground Cabinet War Rooms, where Winston Churchill commanded Britain's forces during the Second World War.

The British Museum has collected objects from around the world and put them under one roof. The Rosetta Stone was discovered in Egypt. It is a tablet with three different kinds of writing inscribed on it, including Greek. It gave the French scholar Jean-François Champollion the first clue in trying to decipher the strange system of hieroglyphics, the writing system of the ancient Egyptians.

The museum also holds the Elgin Marbles, which were

taken from Athens by Lord Elgin in 1806. They used to be part of the Parthenon, one of the most important buildings surviving from ancient Greece. Today Greece is very keen to get the stones back, but the British government has refused to let them leave London.

There are fossils galore at the **Natural History Museum**. Some of the very first dinosaurs to be discovered are here. They were found on a beach in Dorset by Mary Anning, a poor beachcomber. The museum has recently opened the Darwin Centre, which is where they store the remains of many different kinds of animals, from insects to giant squids in jars.

The Natural History Museum is right next door to the **Science Museum** and the **Victoria and Albert Museum** (the 'V & A'). The Science Museum has a working model of the very first computer, as well as space rockets, engines, in fact, almost every machine imaginable.

The V & A is a design museum, with examples of everything from how people used to dress in the past to the latest designs for chairs and lamps.

What was it like during the Blitz in London? Have you ever wondered what it was like to live in a trench

in the First World War? The **Imperial War Museum** in Brixton has exhibits on all the major wars of the 20th century.

To find out about the Navy or to learn about the Battle of Britain and fighter planes visit the **National Maritime Museum** in Greenwich and climb aboard *HMS Belfast* to see how a war ship works; or visit the **Royal Air Force Museum** in Hendon to learn about the Battle of Britain and fighter planes.

The **Foundling Hospital Museum** is an exhibition about Sir Thomas Coram's Foundling Hospital, where poor children and orphans lived in the 18th and 19th centuries. The **Ragged School** recreates what it was like to be an orphan in Victorian London.

Clink Street Prison Museum shows what it was like to be on the wrong side of the law in the past. Do you know how Anne Boleyn was beheaded? Do you want to see Jack the Ripper at his ghastly work? The **London Dungeon** is the place to see these vivid scenes from the dark side of the city's history.

Other Attractions

Built for the Millennium, the **London Eye** is the largest wheel in the world. It weighs 1,600 tonnes and stands 130 metres (435 feet) high. It takes half an hour for the 32 capsules to rotate a full circle. In 2002 it was the most popular attraction in London, with more than 15,000 visitors every day!

Why are there **blue plaques** nearly everywhere in London? The blue plaques were started more than 100 years ago to commemorate the lives of famous people who once lived in the city. Today there are about 700 plaques on buildings that were once the homes of people such as Charles Dickens, Sigmund Freud, Jimi Hendrix, John F. Kennedy and Karl Marx.

Have you ever wanted to look the Queen in the face, stand next to Tom Cruise, sing with Kylie Minogue or try your hand at *Pop Idol*? At **Madame Tussaud's** on Marylebone Road wax models of the famous and infamous can be found. Madame Tussaud was a Frenchwoman who fled to England, fearing the guillotine of the French Revolution. The English were astounded by her lifelike models of executions and murders. They are still very popular today.

Tower Bridge is one of the great symbols of London. It is the most easterly bridge crossing the Thames. It was built in the 19th century, when the Port of London was still working and large ships had to sail into the city. On special occasions the bridge still lifts up to let a tall ship enter London.

The **Monument** was built close to the street where the Great Fire of London began on 2 September 1666. It was designed by Christopher Wren, who was also in charge of rebuilding St Paul's. The Monument is the tallest free-standing column in the world, 61 metres (202 feet) high. The golden urn on the top was originally removable. Wren designed the column so that it could be used as a massive telescope.

The ***Cutty Sark***, moored at Greenwich, is the last

complete example of a 'tall ship' from the 19th century. It was built to bring tea back from China around the Cape of Good Hope, South Africa. It was built to sail as fast as possible, because the ship that arrived back in London first always got the best price for the tea it brought.

Royal Palaces

Before Buckingham Palace became the main home of the royal family, there were many other palaces in or near London that were home to kings and queens.

Did you know that **Kensington Palace** used to be outside London? It started as a hunting lodge for Charles I. The present building was designed for William III and his wife Mary II, but it was never finished properly, as they moved to Hampton Court instead. It is most famous today as the last home of Princess Diana.

Henry VIII went to his palace at **Hampton Court** by boat along the Thames. It was also the favourite home of William and Mary, who built a very famous garden there, including the maze. After a recent fire it has been renovated and it is possible to see how royal families lived hundreds of years ago.

Richmond Park was first designed by Charles I as a hunting park. He enclosed the area and filled it with deer. The deer are still there today, but now they are protected against any hungry hunter. The park also contains the Royal Ballet School.

Greenwich used to be the centre of the Royal Navy. Today the National Maritime Museum can be found inside the palace that Christopher Wren designed for Charles II. When his niece Mary became queen she turned it into a hospital. It is still one of the most remarkable buildings in London. Greenwich also used to be the site of the Royal Observatory, where Greenwich Mean Time was set. You can still see the observatory buildings there.

Fabulous Buildings and Sights

Castles

Thousands of years ago fortifications were built at **Maiden Castle** in Dorset by Iron Age settlers. Nothing remains of their wooden castle, but the deep ditches and gullies that they cut into the side of the hill suggest what a formidable fortress it must have been.

Windsor Castle was built on a hill above the Berkshire town, to give the defenders as good a view as possible. It was built by William the Conqueror to help in the protection of London. The central round tower with its jagged top is the oldest part, dating back to 1080. Today the castle is still one of the royal family's homes. Did you know that it is the longest-inhabited castle in Europe?

Northumbria, the region of England that used to be under threat of invasion from Scotland, has the largest number of castles in the country. **Bamburgh Castle** used to be the home of an Anglo-Saxon king, Ida the Flamebearer. The castle survived numerous sieges during the War of the Roses, but as this threat died away the castle became neglected. It was restored in the 19th century by Baron Armstrong, who had made his money as an industrialist.

Leeds Castle, near Maidstone in Kent, also started as a Norman castle. It was given to Edward I by one of his knights in 1278 and has been rebuilt several times. The castle is surrounded by a protective moat, which makes it look, today, more like a fairy-tale castle than a fortress. This is perhaps why Henry VIII gave it to his many wives, rather than using it for his army.

Arundel Castle is the home of the dukes of Norfolk, who are members of the leading Catholic family in England, the Howards. The original Norman castle, set high on a hill like Windsor Castle, was destroyed during the English Civil War (1642–49). The old castles were no longer any defence against cannon. It was rebuilt taking in some of the old castle but also adding a new family house.

The last castle to be built in England is **Castle Drogo**, the fantasy country home built for a millionaire, Julius Drewe, between 1910 and 1930. It was designed by the English architect Sir Edwin Lutyens and is located in the middle of wild Dartmoor, Devon. Using many of the features you would find in a medieval castle, Drogo is also a country house with every convenience provided, including a croquet lawn, electricity, a library and a garage!

The English Village

The parish priest, usually called the vicar or the rector, used to be one of the most powerful men in each English village. Every year each farmer had to give one tenth of his harvest to the church. It was called a tithe. This made the church wealthy, which explains why village churches, as well as vicarages or rectories, are usually such impressive buildings.

Many villages have more than one pub and some are very old. Old pubs can have very strange names that can derive from almost anything. The King's Head is usually in memory of the executed Charles I; the Eagle and Child, a common pub name in northern England, comes from the badge of the earls of Derby, who owned lots of land in this region.

The manor is where the most important family in the village used to live. The 'lord of the manor' is an ancient position that's no longer in use today. Many of the finest manor houses were built during the reigns of Henry VIII and Elizabeth I.

Yew hedges were grown around village cemeteries, not to hide the graves but because yew wood makes the best bows and arrows. England's victories in its wars with France in the Middle Ages are often credited to the skill of English archers.

There is sometimes now a sports or cricket field on the village green. This used to be called the common and everyone was allowed to feed their animals here. Most villages hold a summer fête or a flower show on the green.

Cathedrals

In Anglo-Saxon times, a city was defined not just because it was where the king lived, but also because there was a cathedral. These buildings sometimes took hundreds of years to be built. The intricate details of the carvings could take generations to complete.

Alfred the Great made **Winchester** the capital of Wessex. It was then the capital of the whole of England until William the Conqueror moved to London. Winchester Cathedral was built on a marsh, so that the whole building was actually floating. This was not a very safe way to build. In 1906 a deep-sea diver, William Walker, began the job of laying cement bags under the building. He worked for six hours a day in his diving suit and it took him five years to finish.

Ely Cathedral in Cambridgeshire was started in 1083 and took 368 years to complete. It was built by the Normans, partly in celebration of the defeat of the last Anglo-Saxon rebel, Hereward the Wake.

Canterbury was the first site for a cathedral. It is still the premier church in England. It was here in 1170 that the Archbishop Thomas Becket was murdered by four knights after he had quarrelled with the king, Henry II. Becket was made a saint and a shrine to him was built inside the cathedral. This shrine is the destination for Geoffrey Chaucer's pilgrims in *The Canterbury Tales* (see p.38).

Before pilgrims went to worship at Canterbury, **Durham** Cathedral was the most important site for religious travellers. It is here that the remains of St Cuthbert are kept. It is said that, after his death, his body stayed intact, without rotting. The last examination, in 1899, sadly revealed that he was just dust and bones. The church also contains the tomb of the Venerable Bede (672–735), the man who wrote the first history of England.

Salisbury Cathedral was built in the 13th century. It took only 40 years to build. It is distinctive for its spire, which soars to 123 metres (404 feet) and is the tallest in England. The builders were warned not to build a spire so high, as it would collapse. It survived until the 1670s, when Christopher Wren ingeniously devised a way to make the spire safe.

York Minster is the second most important cathedral in England and the largest church in northern Europe. Work on the present building started in the 13th century and was not completed until 1474. It is famous for its stained-glass windows. The Rose Window celebrates the marriage of Henry VII and Elizabeth of York in 1486. This marriage brought the War of the Roses to an end (see p.24).

Liverpool's Catholic Cathedral was started in 1962. It was built on the site of the largest Victorian workhouse in England. This was like a prison where the poor used to be sent when they could no longer work. The cathedral is a very modern building that some say looks like a spaceship.

Theme Parks

These are the five most popular theme parks in England.

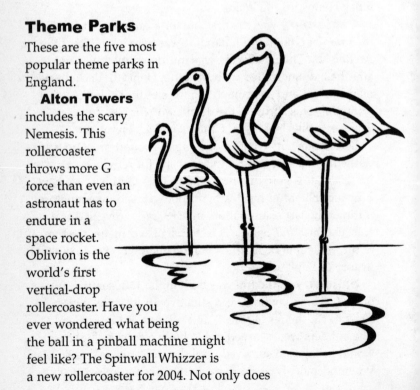

Alton Towers includes the scary Nemesis. This rollercoaster throws more G force than even an astronaut has to endure in a space rocket. Oblivion is the world's first vertical-drop rollercoaster. Have you ever wondered what being the ball in a pinball machine might feel like? The Spinwall Whizzer is a new rollercoaster for 2004. Not only does it twist and turn, but it also spins like a top.

Blackpool Pleasure Beach is the country's most popular free attraction, with more than seven million visitors a year. There are 145 rides, including the biggest and fastest rollercoaster in Europe, the Pepsi Max Big One. Its cars reach 235 feet above the ground and move at speeds up to 87 miles per hour. Grand National, built in 1935, was the first wooden rollercoaster in England.

Thorpe Park is the nearest theme park to London. The park combines a history park and thrilling rides. The newest and scariest rides are Colossus, which has 10 complete gravity-defying loops; and Nemesis Inferno, which is similar to the Alton Towers ride but is built around a volcano!

Drayton Manor began in 1949 and has a variety of different types of family rides. Maelstrom is a pendulum ride: the cars flip upside down and spin around at the same time.

Flamingo Land is also a zoo. The G force on Wall's Magnum Force is a massive five, the largest in the UK. Cliff Hanger is a free-fall nightmare, with a vertical drop of 120 feet.

Zoos and Safari Parks

London Zoo, in Regent's Park, is the oldest public zoo in Europe. It was opened in 1847. The Zoo is also an important scientific centre. Of the 650 species exhibited, 112 are seriously endangered.

Longleat House in Wiltshire is one of the finest stately homes in England. The lions of Longleat have been there since 1966. Be careful not to get out of your car during the drive-through safari, which takes a journey through a series of landscapes where giraffes, zebras, gorillas, buffalo and camels roam free.

Whipsnade Open Zoo was created during the 1930s to house some of the animals from London Zoo. It used to be a

farm and spreads over more than 600 acres. The first animals to arrive were eight birds, which were then joined by a wombat and a skunk. Today the zoo is home to more than 2,500 animals, from spiders to elephants.

It is not difficult to guess what is at **Birdworld** in Surrey. It is the largest bird park in Britain. There are also a petting zoo and an aquarium.

The **National Aquarium** in Plymouth, Devon, is England's largest and also contains the largest water tank in Europe. Do you know what the fish eat every day? They get a daily meal of 36 lettuces, 20 kg of prawns, 30 kg of squid, 30 kg of mackerel, 15 kg of mussels and 15 kg of fish pellets!

Stately Homes

The rich did not only live in castles. They also built impressive country houses. From the basic village manorhouse to huge ornate palaces, the more powerful a family was, the bigger the house had to be!

Hardwick Hall was built by Bess of Hardwick, who became rich by marrying four times! In those days glass was very expensive, but Bess was so rich that she decided to build a house with so many windows that it looks as if the whole building is made of glass For houses of a similar period see also Hatfield House, near St Albans in Hertfordshire; Audley End House, Essex; and Blickling Hall, Norfolk.

Do not be taken in by the name **Castle Howard**. It is in fact a stately home, built in the 18th century by Sir John Vanbrugh and Nicholas Hawksmoor for the Howard family. By that time there was no need for castles. The house was built to show how powerful the family was, without any threat of attack. The building has 100 rooms and 500 windows. Every morning the servants have to switch on 83 sets of lights before breakfast.

Chatsworth House in Derbyshire was first built by Bess of Hardwick in 1552, but burned down 150 years later. It was redesigned at the same time as Blenheim Palace to look like a huge Roman villa. It is now one of England's finest and largest country houses. Later, in the 1840s, they even destroyed the neighbouring village of Edensor and rebuilt it on a different site, just so that Chatsworth would have better views over the countryside.

Holkham Hall in Norfolk has been owned by the same family since 1609. It is a typical house of a rich man who had been on the 'Grand Tour', an educational gap year that the sons of the wealthy took to see all the classical sites of France, Italy and Greece. The house is full of art picked up on the continent.

Woburn Abbey is no longer an abbey. In fact, none of the Cistercian monastery exists, because it was destroyed during the reign of Henry VIII, when most church property was confiscated by the crown. The house was built in the mid-18th century for the Russell family, who still own it today. It is also famous for its deer park and safari park.

Waddesdon Manor was built in the 1870s by the incredibly wealthy Rothschild family. It looks as if a French chateau has landed in the middle of the English countryside.

The Rothschilds are a famous banking family but they were also renowned wine growers. There is a suitably large wine cellar in the house!

Haunted Houses

Borley Rectory, near Sudbury, is supposed to be the most haunted house in England. It was built in the 19th century on top of an old priory (a kind of convent). The ghost of a nun, who was punished for trying to escape by being walled up in the cellar, is said to have been the first spooky visitor.

The next family to live there heard whispering voices, footsteps, pebbles being thrown and the ringing of bells. When the famous ghost hunter Harry Price came to investigate, he was attacked by objects flying across the room.

Then the house was finally destroyed in a mystery fire. The story goes that, as people came to try and fight the fire, a ghostly figure appeared at an upstairs window, staring out at them.

There are many other houses, churches and castles in England that are said to be haunted. Here are a few of the most scary.

Sanford Orcas Manor, near Sherbourne in Dorset, is said to be the home of more than 10 ghosts. A spectral footman is said to have bothered the servants and there is a story of a priest who tried to smother guests with his cloak while they were asleep.

Featherstone Castle in Northumberland is home to a chilling wedding story. The day before the wedding of Baron Featherstonehaugh's daughter, the guests went on a hunt, where they were ambushed and killed. Some say that on the anniversary the wedding party can be seen riding towards the castle on ghostly horseback.

The Beach

As Great Britain is an island, you are never too far from miles of beaches. There are a lot to choose from: sandy swimming beaches, small coves and inlets, surfing beaches, rock-pool paradises, or even bleak shingle that runs down to crashing waves.

The seaside resorts began in the mid-18th century, when doctors began to tell their patients that sea air and swimming were good for practically every illness. Many resorts, such as Brighton, Weymouth and Blackpool, began as resorts for the rich. But with the arrival of trains and cheaper travel in the 19th century the seaside become the ideal destination for everyone.

Many resorts built piers as attractions to lure more visitors. The 19th century saw piers being built all around the country. Some are still in use today, but some, like the resort towns themselves, have become victims of the changing times. Many of the piers are now considered

The Country Code

There are certain things to watch out for when you are in the countryside. This is the Country Code.

☞ Do not light a fire anywhere, especially on beaches.

☞ When you have passed through a gate, always remember to shut it. You don't want all the cattle to escape!

☞ Use the public footpaths when crossing farmland.

☞ Take your litter home. The hedgerows are home to many different types of animals, not chocolate wrappers!

☞ Do not make too much noise. You may not be able to see the wildlife, but that does not mean that it is not there.

☞ If you are climbing over a gate, always climb over near the hinge, rather than near the bolt end.

☞ Farm machinery can be very dangerous. Do not use it as a climbing frame.

historic buildings and efforts are being made to preserve them.

It is also possible to find a quiet beach where one can sunbathe, swim and beachcomb, searching the sand and rock pools for strange shells and sea life. Crabs, scallops, mussels and starfish can all be found in summer. There are many places around the country where you can find seal colonies or coastal birds.

Around England in a Jiffy

The South Coast

In 1940, when Germany invaded France, 338,000 Allied soldiers were stranded across the Channel, in Dunkirk. A fleet of small boats, from fishing vessels to yachts was launched from Dover and the nearby ports to collect the soldiers off the beach, in an impossibly courageous expedition that delivered them home to England.

The 'Cinque Ports' was the name given to the five ports that were closest to France: Sandwich, Dover, Hythe, Romney and Hastings. In the Middle Ages these towns were commanded to develop a navy to defend the country. Rye, not originally one of the Cinque Ports, was added to the list in 1287. A fortified wall with four towers was built. The town was frequently attacked by the French and was destroyed in 1377. It is now considered one of the prettiest towns in England, with its cobbled streets and quaint houses.

Brighton was England's first seaside resort. It was so popular that it used to be known as 'London by the Sea'. The young Prince George (who later became George IV) was a big fan of Brighton and built the absurd Royal Pavilion here to entertain his friends, along with his wife Mrs Fitzherbert, whom he had secretly married. The Pavilion is a lavish home, a bit like a wedding cake, decorated to look like an Indian palace. It was completed in 1822 by John Nash (see p.74).

For less regal visitors to Brighton the two piers were built in Victorian times. The Palace Pier and the West Pier both had amusement arcades and concert halls. The West Pier

The Southeast: Keep your eyes peeled

The Southeast of England has a lot of gentle scenery and is perfect for arable farming. It is also so close to London that many people live in the countryside and commute to the city.

The long coastline, which includes the White Cliffs of Dover, is dramatic. Because it is the closest point to the continent, it is also called the 'invasion coast' and has seen attacks from France, Holland and Spain (but not recently). Today it is better known for the popular beach resorts of Brighton, Hove and Eastbourne.

Here are the top 10 things to do in the Southeast.

1. Pretend to be a prince at Brighton Royal Pavilion

2. Punt along the Cam at Cambridge

3. Cycle around the dreaming spires of Oxford

4. Walk like a Roman at Colchester

5. Live the aristocratic life at Blenheim Palace

6. Return to prehistoric England at Stonehenge

7. Become a pilgrim at Canterbury Cathedral

8. Fight alongside Nelson on HMS *Victory*

9. Defend England against the French at Rye and the other Cinque Ports

10. Mess about on boats on the Isle of Wight

was once England's finest pier, but it was burned down and is now slowly falling into the sea.

East Anglia

East Anglia is in constant battle with the sea. Some parts of it are so flat and low-lying that they are below sea level. Before the surrounding land was irrigated, Ely Cathedral was built on an island encircled by marshes. The Suffolk coast is eroding even today.

When the Romans invaded in 43 AD, they named Colchester (Camulodunum) as their first capital. They built a massive wall around the town after Boudicca had burned the city to the ground in 60 AD. The Normans also made Colchester a major centre and built a castle there. The town was besieged for 11 weeks during the English Civil War and the townspeople were so hungry that they ate everything they could, even the rats!

In the Middle Ages East Anglia was the centre of the wool trade, which was how England first became wealthy. Until the 16th century Norwich was the second largest city in England, after London, but with the rise of foreign trade Bristol soon became more important and Norwich declined.

The north Norfolk coast is an Area of Outstanding Natural Beauty, according to the government. The sand dunes that stretch between Holkham, Wells-next-the-Sea, Blakeney and Cromer are home to wildlife. There is even a colony of seals at Blakeney. Wells-next-the-Sea is in fact 1.5 km (1 mile) from the sea! The channels and the port were blocked by sand and tide over the past 300 years.

University Towns

Oxford University was started in 1167, when a group of English students had to flee France for their lives. Cambridge University was founded in 1209 by a group of students who wanted to flee from Oxford! Oxford and Cambridge are the two oldest universities in England. Together they are called 'Oxbridge'.

Salisbury Plain

The first evidence of building at Stonehenge dates from more than 5,000 years ago! It took another 1,000 years to

The facts about Cambridge University

☞ There are 30 colleges in Cambridge.

☞ The Backs is the name given to the land behind some of the colleges that looks onto the River Cam.

☞ In summer punting is a very popular way to see the Backs. A punt is a flat boat. Someone standing on the helm of the boat can use a pole to push the boat along, like a gondolier in Venice.

☞ Most of the colleges are built around square courts. This is because they used to be religious foundations and were designed like monasteries. They have been rebuilt since then, but the original shapes have remained.

☞ Famous students and teachers at Cambridge have included Ernest Rutherford, who split the atom; Isaac Newton; and Charles Darwin. It is no surprise the place has a reputation for science and technology. The famous scientist Stephen Hawking is Professor of Mathematics there.

complete Stonehenge. It is the oldest human structure still standing in Europe.

There are in fact three sites at Stonehenge. The large ditch and outer bank were cut in about 3000 BC. Evidence of a wooden henge and the burnt bodies of about 240 people from a few hundred years later suggest that this was a crematorium. Around 4,500 years ago they began to build the stone circles.

The stone was cut in South Wales and was probably dragged 400 km (250 miles) overland. This was even before the invention of the wheel, so they had to use logs as rollers. There are 80 stones in the outer bluestone ring. The inner

☞ Today there are 35 colleges in Oxford. Two of them are exclusively for women.

☞ Oxford University has its own policemen called 'bulldogs', who wear bowler hats.

☞ The different colleges have very odd names. Most of them are named after saints or rich benefactors, but Brasenose is named after a doorknocker. Magdalen College is pronounced 'Maudlin'.

☞ Oxford has had some very famous teachers: Lewis Carroll, author of *Alice in Wonderland*, was a maths teacher; Christopher Wren was a professor of Astronomy; J.R.R. Tolkien taught early English literature; and William Buckland, a famous geologist, was known as the man who tried to eat every kind of animal in the world, served dormice at supper and had a jackal in his sitting room.

☞ The very first museums were collections of strange things kept in special display boxes called 'cabinets of curiosity'. The oldest in England, Tradescant's Ark, can now be found at the Ashmolean Museum in Oxford. The original collection was owned by John Tradescant, James I's gardener. It includes Guy Fawkes's lantern, Oliver Cromwell's death mask and other bizarre objects.

horseshoe is made from five trilithons, where two upright stones hold up a horizontal lintel. The only tools the people had at the time were stone axes, bones and wood!

Nobody knows what the stones were used for. One guess is that it is a cosmic clock. On the morning of the summer solstice, the longest day of the year, the Sun rises and hits the site precisely in the middle, as if it was a sun dial.

Old Sarum is the site of an Iron Age fort. The two deep ditches that once surrounded the fort are more than 5,000 years old . The Romans also built a fort there. In the 12th century the inhabitants decided to move. They resettled at Salisbury and built the famous cathedral (see p.87).

Portsmouth and the Isle of Wight

Portsmouth has always been the headquarters of the Royal Navy. There are three very famous ships of the fleet there.

The *Mary Rose* was the flagship of Henry VIII's navy. It was built in 1545, to be used in fighting the French. The ship sailed out of the harbour on its first trip, turned and capsized, with 700 men on board. The ship was not recovered until the 1980s. Since then many artefacts from the *Mary Rose*, such as the sailors' clothes and armour, have helped us to understand what life was like in the 16th century.

HMS *Victory* was the ship that Horatio Nelson captained

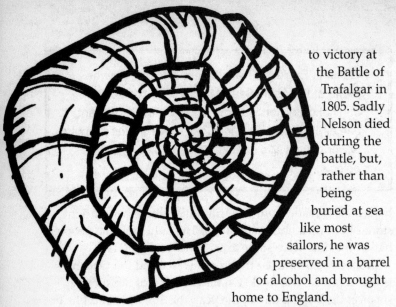

to victory at the Battle of Trafalgar in 1805. Sadly Nelson died during the battle, but, rather than being buried at sea like most sailors, he was preserved in a barrel of alcohol and brought home to England.

HMS *Warrior* was the first 'ironclad' boat of the Royal Navy. It had a thick iron hull that could withstand normal cannon. It was powered by both sail and steam power. It is a shame that in its 22-year career it never once fired a shot!

Across the Solent from Southampton is the Isle of Wight. The island is very popular among sailors. Every August there is the Cowes Regatta, a series of races that attracts some of the best boats in the world. Queen Victoria was also a fan of the island more than 150 years ago. She built a summer house, Osborne House, here. When her husband died she came here to mourn and stayed so long that the Prime Minister, Benjamin Disraeli, had to beg her to return to London.

Wessex

In 1810 Mary Anning from Lyme Regis, found the bones of a very strange animal in the cliffs. Her discovery began the fashion for fossil-collecting. This hunt led to the scientific investigation of dinosaurs. All along this Dorset coast fossil-

In 2002 more than 20 million British tourists and 1.5 million overseas tourists visited the West Country. The region is most famous for its beautiful rural landscapes and dramatic coastline.

This includes two National Parks, Exmoor and Dartmoor, that cover more than 1,631 sq km. There are also almost 4,600 sq km of Areas of Outstanding Natural Beauty, including 400 km of coastline.

Devon and Cornwall have the mildest weather in England. Because of the Gulf Stream and the warm air, spring comes earlier and summer lasts longer in this region.

Here are the top 10 things to do in the West Country:

1. Play James Bond at the Eden Project
2. Take a dip at the Roman Baths in Bath
3. Become a knight at King Arthur's Round Table in Cornwall
4. Search for the witch at Wookey Hole
5. Surf the waves at Newquay
6. Hunt for fossils at Lyme Regis
7. Come face to face with the Cheddar Man at Cheddar Gorge
8. Beat the tide at St Michael's Mount
9. Search for the Hound of the Baskervilles on Dartmoor
10. Clamber up Glastonbury Tor

hunters have chipped away at the cliffs, hoping to find the next ichthyosaur. Unfortunately, Mary Anning never made any money from her discovery. Her grave can be found in the churchyard at Lyme Regis.

It is not just Salisbury Plain that has a spooky past.

Glastonbury Abbey used to be one of the richest in Europe. Today it is in ruins. The town used to be called Avalon and there are many legends surrounding the place. It is said to have been here that King Arthur and his queen Guenevere died. Even stranger still is the story that the Tor may be the last resting place of the Holy Grail, a cup brought here by Jesus's uncle, Joseph of Arimathea, who is said to have set up the first church in 63 AD.

Nearby is Wookey Hole, which has enough natural curiosities to give some people goose pimples. The underground caves are full of the strangest rock formations. In 1904, when the caves were discovered, they found the bones of cavemen and hyenas, and even the twisted body of an old woman who has been called the Witch of Wookey Hole. Some people say that she still haunts the caves.

The remains of a man who lived 9,000 years ago were found at Cheddar Gorge. This deep ravine, which runs for 150 metres (500 feet), was created in the Ice Age. Many of the caves have been used by local farmers to store cheese. This is where the famous Cheddar cheese originates from.

Bath and Wells

The natural springs of Bath have been a fashionable place to visit since before Roman times. The Romans named the town Aquae Sulis, which means 'the waters of Sulis', the Celtic goddess of water. It was popular for more than 400 years. It is still possible today to see some of the ancient ruins. The spring produces 1 million litres of water at a constant 48° C every day!

Queen Anne visited Bath in 1702 and soon the town was revived and developed as a resort.

Jane Austen, the famous author of *Pride and Prejudice*, was a regular visitor and wrote many novels that feature Bath. *Northanger Abbey* involves a ball at the Assembly Rooms;

much of the romance of *Persuasion* occurs there, including a meeting at the famous Pump Room. It was an ideal place for a young woman to find a husband. Austen, who never married, hated the place!

Wells, just outside Bath, is the smallest city in England. Its population is only 9,000, but it has a magnificent cathedral, which was completed in the 13th century. On the front of the building there are more than 300 statues and several alcoves. On special holidays choirboys used to stand in the alcoves or behind statues and sing during processions.

Bristol

In the 17th century Bristol became the second largest city in England after London. It was the main western port for the country and the first port of call for many ships.

It was from here that John Cabot set off on his voyage from England to discover Newfoundland (now in Canada), five years after Columbus discovered the Americas in 1492.

The Corn Exchange was not just the place where they sold corn. This was the building where everything from the rest of Europe, and from Asia, Africa and the Americas, was traded, from sugar to cod. The current building was built in 1735 and used to be the most important building in the city.

Bristol remained an important town during the Industrial Revolution, the great engineer Isambard Kingdom Brunel did much of his work here.

SS *Britain*, which sits at the Bristol docks, was the very first iron-hulled, steam-driven liner that travelled across the Atlantic. Launched in 1833, it travelled 32 times around the world.

Clifton Suspension Bridge was also designed by Brunel. It was completed in 1864. It spans 214 metres (702 feet) and is 75 metres (245 feet) above the River Severn. Four million cars cross the bridge every year.

You won't notice it unless you travel by train, but Brunel also built the Great Western Railway, which connnected Bristol to Paddington Station in London. It was 118 miles long. Parts of it are still being used today, including the longest railway tunnel in England, at Box.

Devon

Sir Arthur Conan Doyle set his most famous Sherlock Holmes novel, *The Hound of the Baskervilles*, on Dartmoor. It is one of the scariest places in England. It is so scary that they put a prison right in the middle of it. Perhaps they were thinking that if the prisoners looked out of their windows they would not want to escape!

The coast of Torbay, which includes Torquay, Paignton and Brixham, is called the 'English Riviera'. The three towns have been popular seaside resorts since the 19th century. In 1688 the last invasion of England occurred at Brixham, when the Dutch King William landed there. It was called the Glorious Revolution, perhaps because nobody was killed and William had actually been invited to take the English throne.

The port of Dartmouth has been home to the Naval College since 1905. Prince Philip, the Duke of Edinburgh, and two of his sons, Prince Charles and Prince Andrew, all trained here.

Although most of the history books say that the *Mayflower* left from Plymouth to take settlers to Massachusetts, in fact it left from Dartmouth harbour. According to legend, near Dittisham, outside Dartmouth, Francis Drake smoked one of the first cigars ever seen in England. His servant thought that he was on fire and poured a bucket of water over him!

Cornwall

Cornwall used to be separate from England. It was never conquered by the Romans and few Anglo-Saxons settled there, so that it was independent from England when William the Conqueror invaded in 1066. Today the Prince of Wales is also the Duke of Cornwall.

Land's End is the furthest point west in England. The rough Cornish coastline, with its tiny coves, is famous for tales of smuggling. Some estimates say that during the Napoleonic Wars more than 100,000 people were involved in the illegal importing of goods. Some smugglers even made ships run aground on the rocky shore in order to steal their cargo.

Camelot, the legendary castle of King Arthur and his Knights of the Round Table, is said by some to have been in Cornwall. The place where the magic sword Excalibur was given back by Arthur to the Lady of the Lake may have been either on Bodmin Moor or on Lizard Point.

The most popular attraction in Cornwall was also used in the recent James Bond film *Die Another Day*. The Eden Project is an extraordinary series of 'biomes' that houses many flowers and other plants from around the world. The Eden Project was built in an old clay quarry and the biomes are the biggest in the world. The Tower of London could fit inside the largest one!

Just off the coast of Cornwall is St Michael's Mount, which you can reach only at low tide. For the rest of the day the island is cut off. Over the years the buildings on it have been an Iron Age shrine, a Norman monastery, a Tudor fort and a stately home. But be careful not to stay too long and get cut off by the sea!

Stratford upon Avon

Stratford upon Avon is the most popular tourist destination outside London. It was the birthplace of William Shakespeare. But who was Shakespeare? For such a famous man very little is known about his life.

Shakespeare was born in Stratford in 1564 and died there in 1616. His father, John, was a tradesman. William went to school in Stratford and, at the age of 18, married Anne Hathaway. The legend says that he had to flee Stratford when he was caught poaching and it is suggested that he ran away with a travelling theatre group. He finally arrived in London.

Did Shakespeare actually write all 38 of his plays? Many people believe that no one could have written so many masterpieces. Is this jealousy? Some people say that Shakespeare was a pseudonym for other writers, perhaps Francis Bacon, or Christopher Marlowe, or even a member of the royal family!

It is said that most people use about 15,000 words in conversation. Shakespeare used more than 29,000!

Both Elizabeth I and James I were fans of his plays. But that does not mean to say that they are not also very funny and sometimes very rude. He wrote as much for the rich as for the 'groundlings'. They were the poor spectators who came to the theatre but could not afford a seat, so they stood on the ground in front of the stage and usually shouted abuse at the actors!

During the 19th century the Midlands was the powerhouse of the world. This is where the modern industrial world began. Goods from everywhere you can think of were delivered to the English ports and sent by canal or rail to the factories, where they were made into things to buy.

Today the Midlands is still a hard-working region. One in every three British cars are made here and a third of all UK jewellery is made within a mile of Birmingham.

Here are the top 10 things to do in the Midlands:

1. 'To be or not to be' in Stratford upon Avon

2. Check out the chocolate at Bournville

3. Live the aristocratic life at Chatsworth House

4. Walk across the iron bridge at Ironbridge

5. Discover a world of industry at ThinkTank

6. To infinity and beyond at the National Space Centre

7. Come face to face with the Plague at Eyam

8. Play *Cider with Rosie* at Painswick

9. Work the cotton mill at Quarry Mill

10. Search for Robin Hood at Nottingham Castle

Did you know that Shakespeare never published his own work? The first printed version of his plays, the First Folio, was published after his death by two actors who edited his work. It is full of mistakes!

The Cotswolds and Cheltenham

The Cotswolds is an area of idyllic towns and villages set in very picturesque landscape. The area made its fortune in the Middle Ages from wool and was almost untouched by the Industrial Revolution, preserving its beauty almost by accident.

Chipping Campden was built on the wealth of the wool trade. It is also famous as the centre of the Arts and Crafts movement, a band of artists who hated the Industrial Revolution. In 1902 Charles Ashby moved 70 London labourers to the town to learn traditional crafts and 'improve themselves'. It was a disaster, as nobody wanted to buy their expensive work when factories were producing similar things far more cheaply. The experiment lasted for only six years.

Dover Hill, near Chipping Campden, used to be the home of the Cotswold Games, which were banned for being too dangerous. Competitions included shin-kicking! The tradition has been revived, but without all the blood.

The author Laurie Lee is famous for his classic book *Cider with Rosie*. It is a memoir of growing up in the Slad Valley near Painswick and is a wonderful re-creation of a past time, including drinking cider and having a first kiss with Rosie, who was in fact Lee's cousin.

To the west of the Cotswolds is the town of Cheltenham. Cheltenham, like Bath, used to be a very popular spa town. The water from the well used to be bottled as a medicine to cure everything from asthma to worms! Cheltenham is also famous for its horse-racing. The Cheltenham Gold Cup is held in March every year.

The Welsh Marches

The 'Welsh Marches' is a name for Shropshire, Herefordshire and the other counties along the Welsh border. 'Marches' is an old word meaning 'borderlands'.

It seems that the English have often been frightened of attack by the Welsh. In the eighth century Offa, the Anglo-Saxon King of Mercia, built a defence called Offa's Dyke along the Welsh border. It is a long raised bank that dips into a deep ditch. It is still the longest earthwork in the world, running for 240 km (150 miles).

In the Middle Ages the Welsh Marches were ruled by a number of English lords, known as the Marcher Lords, who had the special task of making sure that the Welsh did not invade England. They built a line of castles along the border, including Chester, Shrewsbury, Ludlow, Hereford and Chepstow. They kept their power until Wales and England were united into a single kingdom by Henry VIII.

If there is one place that can be called the birthplace of the Industrial Revolution, it is Ironbridge Gorge near Telford in Shropshire. In 1709 Abraham Darby I discovered a new way of producing iron from iron ore. It was this iron that was used to build many of the early factories, steam engines and railways. In 1781 Darby's grandson, Abraham Darby III, built the western world's first iron bridge, over the River Severn. It is considered so important today that it has been named as a World Heritage Site.

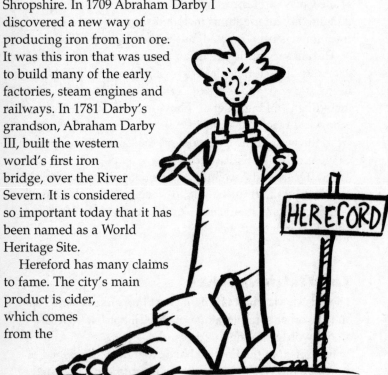

Hereford has many claims to fame. The city's main product is cider, which comes from the nearby apple orchards. In the cathedral is the Mappa Mundi, which was drawn in 1289 and is considered to be the most important medieval map in England. It shows the northern hemisphere of the world – even in the Middle Ages everyone knew that the world was not flat – but with Jerusalem at the centre. The countries shown are a mixture of real and imaginary places. There are even stranger people, including the Sciapod, who has just one enormous foot!

Birmingham

The Industrial Revolution changed Birmingham from a village into 'the city of 1,001 trades'. In 1780 it was still a small market town, but by 1830 the population had trebled to 130,000. Today it is the second largest city in England, with more than one million citizens.

The founding industrialists of Birmingham were called 'the Lunar Men', because they were members of a scientific club called the Lunar Society. They included James Watt, who devised the first working steam engine; Joseph Priestley, who discovered oxygen; the 'button king' Matthew Boulton; Josiah Wedgwood, who developed a way of mass-producing pottery; and Erasmus Darwin, Charles's grandfather. Their club met every month, at the time of the full moon, to discuss new ideas and inventions. Their meeting place is now the Soho House Museum.

There are more canals in Birmingham than in the whole of Venice. Before the railways came, canals were the most practical way to move goods around the country. By 1805 there were 4,800 km (3,000 miles) of waterways in England.

Birmingham is also known as 'Brum' and the locals are called 'Brummies'. These words come from the old nickname for the city, 'Brummagem'.

Four miles south of the city centre is Bournville, where the Cadbury family built their chocolate factory. The factory is still the country's largest supplier of sweets.

ThinkTank is a brand new museum that presents the history of science and discovery. Everything in it, from Victorian engines to an IMAX cinema, shows how industry has developed over the past 250 years.

The Industrial Midlands

To the west of Birmingham is the Black Country, which includes the towns of Dudley, Walsall and Wolverhampton. This area got its name because the smoke from the factories used to cover everything in soot.

Leicester, east of Birmingham, has heaps of history. It has Roman origins and nearby is Bosworth Field, where the Wars of the Roses ended in 1485. The city itself is today one of the most diverse in England, with a large Asian community. It also has a number of astronauts! Although a space rocket has never been launched from England, the National Space Centre is very keen to tell the story of the role played by British people in the space race.

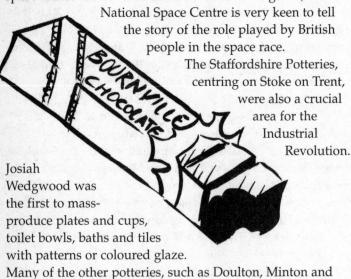

The Staffordshire Potteries, centring on Stoke on Trent, were also a crucial area for the Industrial Revolution. Josiah Wedgwood was the first to mass-produce plates and cups, toilet bowls, baths and tiles with patterns or coloured glaze.

Many of the other potteries, such as Doulton, Minton and Spode, still exist today. Did you know that English bone china used real powdered animal bones to strengthen it?

The other industry that fuelled the Industrial Revolution was cotton. At Quarry Bank Mill in Cheshire there still stands an early cotton mill built by Samuel Greg in 1784. Raw cotton was shipped to Manchester from North America and India, where it was turned into material to be sold around the world. Much of the work was done by orphans, who were brought here from workhouses around the country. By the 1840s there were more than 1,000 children working here.

Nottingham and the East Midlands

Althrop, near Northampton, has been the home of the Spencer family for more than 500 years. It is now the last resting place of Diana, Princess of Wales. She is buried on an island in the centre of the lake, set in a garden designed by Le Nôtre, who also designed the gardens of the Palace of Versailles in France.

Nottingham was once a famous Anglo-Saxon town, but it was completely rebuilt during the Industrial Revolution. Only a few of the old buildings remain, such as the castle on the rock, which is full of hidden passageways. The city also claims to have the oldest pub in England, the 'Trip to Jerusalem', which is said to have first opened its door in 1189.

Robin Hood may not have actually existed, but Nottingham Castle was the last stronghold of Bad King John when his brother Richard the Lionheart returned from the Crusades to retake the throne. Richard had to defeat the sheriff, who was severely punished before Richard spent a few days hunting in Sherwood Forest (which has now been mostly destroyed).

North of Nottingham is the Peak District of Derbyshire, which was named as the first National Park in England in 1951. This region is the southern tail of the Pennines, which snake up through northern England all the way to Hadrian's Wall.

Eyam, near Bakewell in Derbyshire, has a grisly history. In 1665 the Plague came to Eyam from London, probably brought by an Eyam merchant returning home. The villagers decided to contain the disease and nobody was allowed to leave. In 14 months 259 people died and there were only 50 survivors. There are many ghoulish monuments to the Plague and even a museum dedicated to the villagers, who succeeded in stopping the Plague from spreading to other places.

Liverpool

Liverpool began as a small fishing village called 'Livpul'. The first docks were built in 1715, and the merchants made fortunes from slavery, tea and sugar. As it became a busy port, the leaders of the city wanted their home to become the Athens of the North. But it was also the main English port of the 'slave triangle' between the Americas, Africa and England, replacing Bristol.

Liverpudlians are also called 'scousers' after lobscouse, the native dish of the city, a stew made from cheap cuts of meat. A lobscouse without meat is called 'blind scouse'. Both types of lobscouse are eaten with pickled red cabbage.

Liverpool was one of the main immigration ports in England. Many Irish people fled here during the potato famine of 1845. It was also the place where many left Europe for a new life in the New World. Five million passengers set off to New York or Australia from the docks of Liverpool between 1830 and 1900.

Liverpool was the birthplace of the Beatles. John, Paul, George and Ringo first played at the Cavern Club, which no longer exists, but many of the shops mentioned in 'Penny Lane', one of their most famous songs, are still there. The band had a total of 17 no. 1 hits. The band is so famous that

People in the North of England are proud to tell you that their region could almost be a different country. Northerners are proud of their no-nonsense approach to life, their sense of humour, the ruggedness of the landscape and the special ways in which they speak.

One Yorkshireman, David Hallamshire, wrote a book called *Yorkshire Bible Stories* to show how the Bible would sound in Yorkshire English. It starts like this:

'When God first started art like, when he were just getting things off ground as it were, there weren't much of owt to talk of. It were just this sort of shapeless stuff floating abart doing nothin.'

Here are the top 10 things to do in the North:

1. Run down the pier on Blackpool Beach

2. Go mad in Manchester

3. Search for Count Dracula at Whitby

4. Fly with the Angel of the North

5. 'Come Together' with the Beatles in Liverpool

6. Become a Roman soldier on Hadrian's Wall

7. Play with 'baby' at the Science and Industry Museum in Manchester

8. Be a Viking at the Jorvik Viking Centre in York

9. Play 'Swallows and Amazons' on Lake Coniston in the Lake District

10. Ferry 'cross the Mersey

they recently renamed the local airport after John Lennon!

In the 1960s music from Liverpool, called the Mersey Beat, was the most popular in the world. 'Ferry 'cross the Mersey' was a song by Gerry and the Pacemakers. The ferry still goes from Liverpool to Birkenhead today.

Manchester and Salford

Manchester used to be known as 'Cottonopolis' or 'Cotton City', as it was the centre of the cotton industry. Today it is probably more famous for its football teams, Manchester United and Manchester City, and for the revival of the city over the past 20 years, particularly its music scene, which has included the Smiths, New Order, the Happy Mondays, the Stone Roses, Oasis and the famous Hacienda night club.

The city has an unsettled history. It was the centre of protests against many of hardships suffered by ordinary working people. These culminated in the Massacre of Peterloo in 1819. After 50,000 protesters had gathered on St Peter's Field to complain about the working conditions in the factories, soldiers on horseback panicked and charged the crowd with their swords. Sixteen people were killed and many more were wounded.

The first major passenger railway in the world was run out from Castlefields by George Stephenson in 1830. Today the nearby rail sheds have been converted into the Science and Industry Museum. It has a new exhibition about the role that the city has played in science. Did you know that one of the very first computers, called 'baby', was built in Manchester in 1948?

Salford is in fact not part of Manchester but a separate city. This is where *Coronation Street*, the longest running television soap in the world, is made.

The industrial past of Salford is

best captured in the paintings of L.S. Lowry, who is famous for his 'matchstick' men and women. The Lowry in  Salford Quays is a very modern museum that holds many of Lowry's works.

The New Imperial War Museum in Salford is the first building in England to be designed by Daniel Libeskind, the architect who is designing the buildings that will replace the World Trade Center in New York (destroyed on 11 September 2001).

Lancashire

Blackpool is the Brighton of the North, a hugely popular seaside resort. Seventeen million visitors come every year to walk the seven miles of sandy beaches or have a ride at Blackpool Pleasure Beach, the most popular free visitor attraction in England (see p.89).

Blackpool began as a resort for rich Manchester merchants in the 18th century. After the railway arrived, in 1846, it became a resort for everybody, in particular drawing factory workers during the 'Wakes Weeks', the seven-day holidays when most of the Lancashire mills used to close down.

Many of the main attractions were built in the Victorian period. The Blackpool Tower was built in 1894. It is 158 metres (518 feet) high. In its day it was the tallest building in England. The Ballroom at the base of the Tower was finished in 1897. The 'Golden Mile' promenade is bisected by the country's first electric tramway, built in 1885 to ferry visitors between the three piers, imaginatively named South Pier, Central Pier and North Pier.

Inland from Blackpool, Lancashire is a rugged county, spotted with sporadic factory towns such as Burnley,

Accrington and Bolton. This was where the cotton, transported from Liverpool and Manchester, was made into cloth.

Yorkshire

Leeds, Bradford and Sheffield were the most important towns for textiles and steel. Sheffield is still England's fourth largest city. It is home to the bizarrely named football team Sheffield Wednesday and was the location for the film *The Full Monty*.

In a recent book called *The Idler Book of Crap Towns*, Hull on the east coast of Yorkshire was called the worst city in the country. The merchants of Leeds made their fortunes by building mills in which workers turned cloth into cheap clothing for everyone to wear. Marks and Spencer, the famous chain of stores, began as a market stall in Leeds in 1884. Today Leeds is the third largest city in England.

North of Bradford, at Saltaire, is proof that not all the factory-owning bosses were cruel and mean to their workers. Sir Titus Salt believed that it was his job not just to make money but to improve people's lives. His factory employed more than 3,000 men who worked at 1,200 wool looms and at one time it was Europe's largest factory, bigger even than St Paul's Cathedral in London.

Haworth has become famous as a place of pilgrimage for fans of the Brontë sisters. Charlotte, the author of the haunting Victorian novel *Jane Eyre*, and Emily, who wrote *Wuthering Heights*, lived with their sister Anne, their brother Bramwell and their father the Reverend Patrick Brontë in Haworth Parsonage deep in the Pennines. Their's was a tragic family story: all four children died young, leaving their father alone. Their house is preserved as a museum exactly as it would have been in the 1840s.

The Yorkshire Dales surround the towns of Skipton and Harrogate, and the cathedral city of Ripon. The Dales are most famous for the three peaks: Pen-y-Ghent (2,277 feet high), Ingleborough (2,372 feet high) and Whernside (2,415 feet high). There is an annual race to run up and down all three in one day.

In the centre of York there is a street called The Shambles and this is probably because it is! The tiny winding medieval street is exactly as it used to be hundreds of years ago. The smallest street in this area has a very strange name, Whip Ma Whop Ma Gate, which actually means 'neither one thing nor another'.

The Jorvik Viking Centre shows how old the city is. The museum is built on the site where a ninth-century Viking settlement was discovered. It was the Viking capital of northern England until the Normans all but destroyed the city, and then rebuilt the castle and the Minster (cathedral) (see p.88).

York was never an industrial centre, but it did become rich through the railways. The 'railway king' George Hudson made sure that many of the most important lines passed through York. Today the National Railway Museum

commemorates the age of steam. It has engines from around the world, from George Stephenson's 'Rocket' to the Japanese 'bullet train'.

The imposing North Yorkshire Moors contain the largest desolate moorland in England. They are not only perfect for walkers who want a challenge, with more than 1,400 miles of footpaths, but are full of ruined abbeys, Roman forts and miles of bare, wind-blasted hills.

Whitby, on the northern coast of Yorkshire, is an ancient fishing town. Its long history has always been connected to the sea. Up on the hill above the town is St Mary's Church, reached by climbing 199 steps. The church was built by ship's carpenters. This journey was also taken by Count Dracula, in Bram Stoker's novel, after his ship had run aground at Whitby.

The Lake District and Carlisle

For centuries people were so frightened by stories about the imposing Lake District, the closest England gets to a mountainous region, that they avoided visiting it at all. The Romans built their roads around the district and the Normans halted at the border towns. The Lakes were not discovered as places of immense beauty and tranquillity until the 18th century.

Many of the places in Cumbria have very strange names. This is because, without the Romans or the Normans changing place names, the original Celtic or Norse names remain. 'Mere' at the end of a name means 'lake'; 'tarn' is a mountain lake; a 'force' is a waterfall; and a 'ness' is a rocky promontory.

Although this area was first written about in the 1750s, the most famous visitors to Cumbria were the Lake Poets, William Wordsworth and Samuel Taylor Coleridge. Wordsworth grew up in Cumbria and guided his friend Coleridge around it in the 1790s. The Lake District seemed to them the exact opposite of the industrial country that much of England had become. Wordsworth moved to Dove Cottage in Grasmere, which is a museum today.

Coniston Water was the original setting of Arthur Ransome's much-loved children's book *Swallows and Amazons*. It was also the fateful location for a series of attempts at the water speed record. Malcolm Campbell was the first to win the prize in 1927, in the first 'Blue Bird'. In 1967 his son, Donald Campbell, was not so lucky in his boat,

'Blue Bird II'. As he attempted to reach 300 miles per hour he hit an object in the water and the boat was destroyed, with Campbell inside.

Carlisle has been on the front line in the wars between England and Scotland so many times that, from the time of William I in 1066 to the reign of James I, starting in 1603, nobody was sure which country it was in! The castle has been besieged numerous times, the last being in 1745, when Bonnie Prince Charlie, who claimed the throne, led a Scottish army against Carlisle.

Newcastle and Gateshead

Newcastle and Gateshead are like two halves of the same city, facing each other over the River Tyne. There are five bridges that link the two together. The newest is the Millennium Bridge, which in 2002 became the first bridge ever to be named as British 'building of the year'. The bridge is built so that it can open in two arcs when a ship enters the port.

Gateshead is famous for its inventors. George Stephenson developed his engine the 'Rocket' here. An early type of

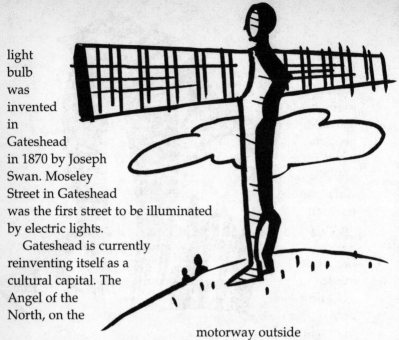

light
bulb
was
invented
in
Gateshead
in 1870 by Joseph
Swan. Moseley
Street in Gateshead
was the first street to be illuminated
by electric lights.

Gateshead is currently
reinventing itself as a
cultural capital. The
Angel of the
North, on the
motorway outside
Gateshead, is the largest sculpture in
Britain. It was designed by the artist Anthony Gormley and
put up in 1996. Its wingspan is wider than a Boeing 767's
and it stands as high as five double-decker buses. The Baltic,
an art gallery opened in 2002 on the quayside, was once a
flour mill.

Grey Street is named after the English Prime Minister
(1830–34) and tea drinker Earl Grey. In 2002 the BBC called
this street the finest street in England. There is a statue of
Earl Grey at the top of the street. It was put up in 1837.
There is a glass time capsule in the bottom, filled with
medals and gold!

The locals are called 'Geordies'. The name goes back to
the time of the Scottish Jacobite rebellion, led by Bonnie
Prince Charlie, in 1745–46. The city was so dependent on the
English crown, then worn by George II, that they resisted
any rebellion and remained George's men!

Newcastle has been voted one of the party capitals of the

world. A night out here is considered to be more fun than even Rio or New York! The partygoers are also known to be some of the hardiest as well. Even in freezing December they walk around in shirt sleeves and won't wear anything but their dancing gear.

Northumbria

North of Newcastle is Hadrian's Wall. The Roman emperor Hadrian visited England in 122 AD and saw that the only way to keep the Scots and the Picts in Scotland was by building a long wall to keep them out. The wall is 115 km (76 miles) long and runs from the Tyne to Bowness on Solway, near Carlisle. It took three legions more than six years to build the wall. There is a fort at every mile and there are two turrets in between each pair of forts. You can still walk along the 10 km (6 miles) of the wall that remain undamaged.

Lindisfarne is one of the most famous Celtic sites in England. It is also known as Holy Island, because it is an important place in religious history. In 635 St Aidan arrived here from Iona and set up a monastery. Later the monks produced the Lindisfarne Gospels, a highly elaborate version of the gospels that is one of the most important handwritten books in the world. To get to the island you have to make sure that it is low tide so that you can walk across. It is not unusual for cars parked on the sand by unknowing visitors to be swept away by the sea at high tide.

Like Carlisle in the west, for centuries Berwick upon Tweed never really decided whether it was Scottish or English. It is the most northerly town in England. The Tweed is, in fact, a river. The Royal Tweed Bridge, which looks like a viaduct but is for the railway, was built by Robert Stephenson, son of the inventor George Stephenson, and opened by Queen Victoria in 1850.

Good Books

Elizabeth Bartsch-Parker and Roibeard O'Maola, *Lonely Planet British Phrasebook* (Lonely Planet)
A valuable guide to the strange words the English use

Nick Brownlee, *Everything You Didn't Need to Know About the UK* (Sanctuary Publishing)
The essential useless facts

Bill Bryson, *Notes from a Small Island* (Doubleday)
One of the most popular books from a very funny travel writer

Terry Deary and Martin Brown, The *Horrible Histories* series (Scholastic)
From *The Terrible Tudors* to the *Frightful First World War*

Robin Eagles, *The Rough Guide History of England* (Rough Guides)
From prehistory to the present day

Farman, John, *The Very Bloody History of London* (Vintage)
Stories about the capital city

Christopher Hibbert, *The Story of England* (Phaidon)
Lots of great pictures from the nation's history

Simon Jenkins, *England's Thousand Best Houses*
Just in case you want to know all about them

Sam Jordison and Dan Kieran (editors), *The Idler Book of Crap Towns: The 50 Worst Places to Live in the UK* (Boxtree)

Ben Schott, *Schott's Original Miscellany* (Bloomsbury)
Crammed full of useless knowledge

W.C. Sellar and R.J. Yeatman *1066 and All That: A Memorable History of England* (Sutton Publishing)
A classic and hilarious look at the history of Britain

Terry Tan, *Culture Shock! Britain* (Graphic Arts Center)
Lots of interesting facts about the English

Lynne Truss, *Eats, Shoots and Leaves: The Zero Tolerance Approach to Punctuation* (Profile Books)
The English obsession with punctuation on display

Wicked Websites

Here are a few general sites that may be useful.

For general information:
www.visitengland.com
www.visitlondon.com
www.cia.gov./cia/publications/factbook/geos/uk.html

For information on stately homes, castles and gardens:
www.nationaltrust.org.uk
www.english-heritage.org.uk
www.stately-homes.com
www.english-nature.org.uk
www.museums.co.uk

For more on history and culture:
www.bbc.co.uk/history
www.britainexpress.com/history

For news and weather:
www.bbc.co.uk
www.meto.gov.uk

Quirks and Scribbles